EMERALD HOME LAWYER

A
PRACTICAL GUIDE TO
OBTAINING PROBATE

Peter Wade

Emerald Publishing

C013731532

Emerald Publishing
Brighton BN2 4EG

ISBN 1903909 62 7

Printed by CATS SOLUTIONS Wiltshire

Cover design by Emerald Graphics

Whilst every effort has been made to ensure that the information
contained within this book is correct at the time of going to
press, the author and publisher can take no responsibility for the
errors or omissions contained within.

CONTENTS

INTRODUCTION

The saying goes that we can avoid everything except death and taxes. Maybe probate has the unique distinction of dealing with both these activities. We cannot avoid death but we can avoid taxes.

The proper regulation of one's estate can certainly minimise inheritance tax and maybe get rid of it entirely.

Life becomes more complicated by the day but it is possible without running up excessive legal fees to prepare a valid will and as an executor to undertake probate of someone's estate without legal help.

My definition of probate is very high-class administration. We are capable of doing it if we follow the checklists assiduously and keep a note of everything we do. If every piece of paper is accounted for and filed properly then probate should not be too difficult.

With the advent of computers, photocopiers, faxes and emails and the Internet these things are more easily undertaken by the organised amateur.

The minimum you will need is
1. Telephone
2. Computer
3. Somewhere to file all the letters.

I have attempted to take you through a typical probate transaction and to supply you with checklists, addresses, telephone numbers, and website addresses and draft letters. I have tried to keep the text uncluttered by keeping the non-essential items to the appendixes. There will be notes in the text where these things can be found.

I purchased my first house by using a book although I did have the advantage of working in the legal department of a local authority. I knew nothing about practical conveyancing. It was a famous consumer association guide and I still have that copy on my shelves even though it was about 33 years ago. I am a great believer in *'how to books'*. They can at the very least take out this mystique of what the professionals try to wrap up as being very complicated indeed.

Wills and probate is not brain surgery but you have to follow a procedure precisely to get it right. You can save thousands in legal fees, which incidentally is doing me out of a job, but I will try and live with the rejection.

WRITING YOUR OWN WILL

Everyone over the age of 18 should make a will. Although in the public's view making a will is a straightforward matter it can have devastating effect if not written and executed properly and also if there is no will.

The safest advice is to always get a competent person to draw up and have a will executed for you. You can then rest assured that your wishes will be carried out in the event of your death.

Also if you execute it whilst you are fit and well there is less likelihood of it being overturned by beneficiaries claiming that you were not competent to do it.

If you are in any doubt about your own ability to draw up and execute a will you should get a solicitor to do it for you. At the very least your beneficiaries will be able to sue the solicitor in the event of him or her being incompetent or your beneficiaries missing out because of negligence. If you draw up a poor will they will only be able to regret for the rest of their lives that you had not taken competent legal advice which comes relatively cheaply for a straightforward will.

I often claim that I would happily pay the solicitor's fee for a will to be drawn up were I to be the beneficiary. So far I have not been called upon to pay up on that promise as no one has indicated that they want to make me a beneficiary.

As a practising probate lawyer I see a lot of heartache amongst families when they think the will has not been drawn up properly or they think they can overturn the will because the testator was not mentally capable.

Unfortunately the chance of inheriting does not bring out the best in people. Also families in those circumstances do not seem to enjoy themselves more than when they are falling out over money. We all believe that it would not happen in our family as we are not so petty and mercenary but in my experience no one is exempt.

We would much rather total strangers get part of the estate than let "undeserving" members of our own family.

Occasionally I get well meaning 'know alls' who say I am not paying your fees as everything will go to the wife when I die. That is partially true but intestacy trusts in favour of the children may arise which can tear apart a family. I suppose this boast is to prove how clever the speaker is.

I counter if I am in a difficult mood by saying: yes you deprive me of my fee but you are taking a risk that in the event of your joint death and intestacy your sister in law will inherit your estate. I have no idea whether the speaker has a sister in law but it usually encourages them to dip into their wallet to pay my fee for a properly drawn up Will.

We all have someone to whom we do not wish to leave our estate even if it's only the taxman. Or, on intestacy, ultimately the State. If you leave it to the cats' home provided it is a charity you save the tax and keep it out of the Chancellor's hands. A satisfying outcome

WHY MAKE A WILL?

If you do not have a will then your estate will be distributed in accordance with the rules of intestacy. Intestacy means when there is no will. A testator is the maker of a will.

Apart from limited circumstances you have freedom to leave your estate to whomever you like unlike some other legal systems such as in France.

You are entitled to go to the stationers and use a will form. The only problem with that is that it may work but any mistake in execution will invalidate your wishes.

Everyone should make a will and think about updating it regularly as your circumstances change.

1

Practical Will Drafting

Revocation of Wills
There are two main ways that you can revoke your will: by writing a new one; a formal declaration of all previous wills, by deliberately destroying the will.

Also the Testator must intentionally destroy the will or order someone else to destroy it in his presence.

There are statutory rules as to revocation of wills, and the most important ones being marriage and divorce.

Inheritance tax
Formerly Death Duties and Capital Transfer Tax, it is now one tax on death - Inheritance Tax.

The current level for Inheritance Tax is £275,000.

Any assets over that amount will be subject to a single rate of Tax of 40%. Therefore the first £275,000 is exempt, thereafter 40%.

If you give away your estate and survive seven years, then no tax will be payable on the estate., There is a sliding scale over the seven-year period from:
0 - 3 years = 100%
3 - 4 years = 80%
4 - 5 years = 60%
5 - 6 years = 40%
6 - 7 years = 20%

Any year a gift made during a persons lifetime which exceeds the annual other special exemptions are known as potentially exempt transfers (PET's). These transfers are exempt from Inheritance Tax if the testator lives more than seven years after the gift, but if the testator dies within the seven year period, they may be brought back into the estate. Therefore they are potentially exempt.

Equalisation of Estates
Transfers upon death between husband and wife are exempt and therefore in tax planning terms, if the whole estate has been left to the surviving spouse, then the £275,000 is 'wasted'. The idea is that each spouse uses their tax-free exemption by leaving at least the amount of the nil rate band directly to their children, or other close relatives.

This can only be achieved if the estate is large enough to allow the surviving spouse to have sufficient to maintain themselves.

Because the nil rate band has not been increased in line with inflation, more and more of the general population who would not normally regard themselves are wealthy are coming within the band, particularly on the second death. There are exemptions which can be applied on an annual and a lifetime basis.

Small Gifts
Any gift to any one person up to the value of £250.00 is exempt.

Expenditure out of Income.
Any gift out of Income which leaves you with enough money to maintain yourself would be exempt.

Gifts in consideration of marriage
There is a limit of £5000 if the donor is the parent of one of the marriage partners, and £2500 if the donor is the grandparent of either of the marriage partners. A gift made by anyone else is

£1000.00. There is an annual exemption of £3000 in each tax year.

These gifts must be made before the wedding ceremony.

Gifts to Charity
These are totally exempt, if left to a registered charity.

Gifts to Political Parties
There is no limit to the amount that can be donated to a political party.

Post Death Planning
DEED OF VARIATION
Within the two year period after the death the will can effectively be rewritten to take advantage of the nil-rate Inheritance Tax band. This is made by Deed of Family arrangement. All the beneficiaries must agree to this.

BUSINESS PROPERTY RELIEF
In order to qualify for business property relief two conditions must be fulfilled

The testator must have owned the business property for at least two years before his death and the business property must fall within the prescribed categories

This will be ascertained by taking professional advice as to the definition of business property.

AGRICULTURAL PROPERTY RELIEF
The owner of agricultural property will receive a relief from inheritance tax if two conditions are fulfilled

The interest must be in agricultural property, which means farmland, or farm buildings used with that land.

It must have been occupied for agricultural purpose for at least two years before his death or owned the property at least seven years before his death during which period it was occupied by someone for agricultural purposes

SUGGESTED PRECEDENT WILL CLAUSES

COMMENCEMENT: Name and address of Testator

This is the last will and testament of me ^^^^^^^ of ^^^^^^^ in the County of ^^^^^-

Formal revocation of all previous wills

I REVOKE all former Wills and Testamentary dispositions made by me-

Funeral arrangements

I WISH that my body be buried/cremated-

Appointment of sole executor who is usually wife/ husband who is also sole beneficiary

I APPOINT my ^^^^ to be my sole Executor/Executrix and I GIVE AND BEQUEATH to ^^^^^ all my property both real and personal whatsoever and wheresoever absolutely

PROVIDED that ^^^^^^ survives me by at least thirty days but if my said ^^^^ shall not so survive me I DIRECT that the remaining clauses hereof shall take effect-

Appointment of executor and alternative executor if first one predeceases

(1) I APPOINT my ^^^^ ("my ^^^^") to be the sole executor ^^^ of this Will but if that appointment fails (because ^^^^ dies before me or before proving the Will or is unable or unwilling to act or for any other reason) I APPOINT ^^^^^^ of ^^^^^^ and ^^^^^^ of ^^^^^ to be the executors and trustees of the Will-

IN THIS WILL and any Codicil to it the expression "my Trustees" means its trustees for the time being or (where the context requires) my personal representatives for the time being-

ANY POWERS given to the trustees of this Will (by the Will or any Codicil to it or by the general law) may be exercised by my Trustees before the administration of my estate is complete and even before a grant or representation has been obtained-

Appointment of professional firm to be executors

NB charging clause

(1) I APPOINT the partners at the date of my death in the firm of ^^^^^^^^^^^^ of ^^^^^^^^^^^^^^^ or the firm which at that date has succeeded to and carries on its practice and I EXPRESS the wish that one and only one of those partners (or if the appointment of ^^^^ fails for any reason to take effect then two and only two of them) shall prove the Will and act initially it its trusts-

(2) IN THIS WILL the expression "my Trustees" means my Executors and Trustees of this Will and of any trust arising under it-

(3) ANY POWERS given to the trustees of this Will (by the Will or any Codicil to it or by the general law) my be exercised by my Trustees before the administration of my estate is complete and even before a grant or representation has been obtained-

Appointment of solicitors

(1) I APPOINT as my Executors and Trustees ^^ and the partners at the date of my death in the firm of ^^^^^^^^^^ of ^^^^^^^^^^ or the firm which at that date has succeeded to and carries on its practice and I EXPRESS the wish that one and only one of those partners (or if the appointment of ^^^^ fails for any reason to take effect then two and only two of them) shall prove the Will and act initially in its trusts-

(2) IN THIS WILL the expression "my Trustees" means my Executors and Trustees of this Will and of any trust arising under it-

(3) ANY POWERS given to the trustees of this Will by the Will or any Codicil to it or by the general law) may be exercised by my Trustees before the administration of my estate is complete and even before a grant or representation has been obtained-

NORMAL APPOINTMENT OF EXECUTORS

(1) I APPOINT ^^^^^^ and ^^^^^ to be the Executors and Trustees of this my Will (hereinafter called "my Trustees)-

(2) IN THIS WILL the expression "my Trustees" means my Executors and Trustees of this Will and of any trust arising under it-

(3) ANY POWERS given to the Trustees of this Will (by the Will or any Codicil to it or by the general law) may be exercised by my Trustees before the administration of my estate is complete and even before a grant has been obtained-

I APPOINT ^^^^^ and his wife ^^^^^ and the survivor of them of ^^^^^^ and any person or persons appointed by him/her/them to act after his/her/their death or incapacity to be the guardians during minority of any children of mine who are the minors at the date of death of the survivor of me and my ^^^^^^_

Specific Legacies including personal chattels

I GIVE AND BEQUEATH all my personal chattels as defined by Section 55(1) (x) of the Administration of Estates Act 1925 unto ^^^^^ absolutely-

I GIVE AND BEQUEATH all my personal chattels as defined by Section 55(1)(x) of the Administration of Estates Act 1925 unto my Trustees Upon Trust to dispose of the same as they in their absolute discretion shall think fit or in accordance with any note or memorandum which may be found amongst my papers at my death-

I GIVE AND BEQUEATH to ^^^^^ such of my personal chattels (as the same are defined by Section 55(1) (x) of the Administration of Estates Act 1925) as ^^^^^ may within two months of the date of my death select and I GIVE AND BEQUEATH all personal chattels remaining after ^^^^ has made ^^^^^ selection or the period for making such selection has expired to ^^^^-

Pecuniary legacies

I GIVE AND BEQUEATH the following specific legacies free of Inheritance Tax other fiscal impositions and of costs of transfer-

(1) ^^^^^^

(2) ^^^^^^

I GIVE AND BEQUEATH the following pecuniary legacies free of Inheritance Tax and other fiscal impositions:-

(1) To ^^^^^^^^ the sum of ^^^^^

(2) To ^^^^^^^^ the sum of ^^^^^

Pecuniary legacies to charities etc

I DECLARE that the receipt of the treasurer or other proper officer for the time being of ^^^^^ shall be a sufficient discharge to my Trustees for any legacy hereby given- *(Not necessary if using STEP provisions)*

(1) WITH REFERENCE to Section 31 of the trustee Act 1925 the words "may in all circumstances be reasonable" shall be omitted from paragraph 1 of subsection 1 and in substitution therefore the words "the Trustees may think fit" shall be inserted and the proviso at the end of subsection 1 shall be omitted-

(2) With reference to Section 32 of the Trustee Act 1925 provision A of subsection 1 shall be deemed to be omitted-

RECEIPT FROM CHARITY

THE RECEIPT of anyone purporting to be the treasurer or other proper officer of any charitable or other body to which any gift is made by (or under any provision of) this Will or any Codicil to it shall be a good discharge to my Trustees for the gift- *(Not necessary if STEP provisions being used)*

UNDERAGE BENEFICIARY

IF any legatee hereunder (whether specific or pecuniary) shall be a minor at my death my Trustees may if they think fit pay transfer or deliver the legacy to such legatee personally or to his parent or guardian and the receipt of such legatee notwithstanding his minority or of such parent or guardian shall be a sufficient discharge to my Trustees for such legacy who shall not be further concerned as to the application thereof-

Residuary estate

I GIVE DEVISE AND BEQUEATH all my real and the residue of my personal property whatsoever and wheresoever not hereinbefore specifically disposed of unto my Trustees upon trust to sell call in and convert the same into money with power to postpone the sale calling in and conversion thereof for so long as they in their absolute discretion shall think fit without being liable for loss-

I GIVE DEVISE AND BEQUEATH all my property both real and personal whatsoever and wheresoever unto my Trustees upon trust to sell call in and convert the same into money with power to postpone the sale calling in and conversion thereof for so long as they in their absolute discretion shall think fit without being liable for loss-

Duties of executors

MY TRUSTEES shall stand possessed of the net proceeds of such sale calling in and conversion as aforesaid and my ready money upon trust to pay thereout my debts funeral and testamentary expenses and all duty and taxes payable by reason of my death and after such payment in trust for my said ^^^^^^^ absolutely and if ^^^^^^^ shall predecease me then in trust for such of my children as shall survive me and attain the age of ^^^^ years and if more than one in equal shares absolutely-

PER STIRPES - Grandchildren taking the share their parent would have received if they had lived.

PROVIDED always that if any of my said children shall predecease me leaving issue living at my death who shall attain the age of ^^^ years such issue shall take by substitution per stirpes and if more then one in equal shares the share of my estate which his hers or their parent would have taken had he or she survived me-

RESIDUARY ESTATE

I GIVE all my property not otherwise disposed of by this my Will unto my Trustees upon trust to sell the same (with power to postpone sale) and out of the moneys to arise from such sale to pay my debts legacies my funeral and testamentary expenses and all duty and taxes payable by reason of my death and TO HOLD the residue of the said proceeds of sale in trust for ^^^^^ for[·] ^^^^^ own use and benefit absolutely-

I GIVE all the residue of my estate (out of which shall be paid my funeral and testamentary expenses and my debts) and any property over which I have at my death any general power of appointment to my Trustees ON TRUST to sell call in and convert into money but with full power to postpone doing so for as long as they see fit without being liable for loss (and such estate and property and the property which currently represents it is referred to in this Will as "the Trust Fund")-

MY TRUSTEES shall hold the Trust Fund ON TRUST:-

(1)   To pay its income to my said wife/husband for his/her life (but contingently on surviving me for twenty eight days and without becoming entitled to the income during that period except in that event) and subject to that :-

(2)   Absolutely for such of my children as are alive at the death of the survivor of my said wife/husband and me and reach the age of ^^^ years and if more than one in equal shares PROVIDED that if any child of mine dies (in my lifetime or after my death) before attaining a vested interest but leaves a child or children alive at the death of the survivor of my said wife/husband my child and me who reach the age of ^^^^ years then such child or children shall take absolutely and if more than one in equal shares so much of the Trust Fund as that child of mine would have taken on attaining a vested interest-

I GIVE DEVISE AND BEQUEATH all the residue of my property both real and personal whatsoever and wheresoever not otherwise disposed of by this my Will and any Codicil hereto unto my Trustees upon trust for sale (with power to postpone such sale) to pay my debts funeral and testamentary expenses pecuniary legacies and all duties and other taxes payable by reason my death and to hold the net proceeds of sale upon trust for such of my children who survive me and attain the age of ^^^^ years and if more than one in equal shares absolutely PROVIDED ALWAYS that if any such child of mine shall die in my lifetime leaving issue who survive me and attain the age of

^^^ years then such issue shall take by substitution and more than one in equal shares per stirpes the share of my residuary estate which such deceased child of mine would have taken had he or she survived me and attained a vested interest under this my Will-

IF the foregoing provisions shall fail then my Trustees shall hold my residuary estate for ^^^^ and ^^^^ or the survivor or survivors of them in equal shares absolutely-

FAILURE OF GIFT / SHARE AND THE BALANCE TO GO TO RESIDUARY ESTATE

IF the trusts hereinbefore declared of and concerning any share of my residuary estate shall fail or determine then from the date of such failure or determination such shares shall accrue and be added to the other shares of my residuary estate in equal proportions and be held upon the like trusts and subject to the like powers and provisions as those affecting such other shares-

SURVIVORSHIP CLAUSE

EVERY person who would otherwise benefit under this Will but who fails to survive me for thirty days shall be deemed to have predeceased me for the purpose of ascertaining the devolution of my estate and the income from my estate during the period of thirty days from my death shall be accumulated and added to capital accordingly-

IN this Will or any Codicil to it the Standard provisions of the Society of Trust and Estate Practitioners (First Edition) shall apply-

Extension of executor's powers

MY TRUSTEES may in extension of the power of appropriation conferred on personal representatives by Section 41 of the Administration of Estates Act 1925 at any time at their discretion appropriate any part of my estate in its then actual condition or state of investments in or towards satisfaction of any legacy or any share in my estate without the necessity of obtain the consent of any person- *(Not necessary if STEP provisions are used)*

IN ADDITION to all other powers conferred by law my Trustees may at any time and from time to time raise the whole or any part of the vested contingent expectant or presumptive share or shares of any beneficiary hereunder and pay the same to or apply the same for the advancement maintenance education or otherwise howsoever for the benefit of such beneficiary-

ANY MONEYS requiring investment hereunder may be laid out in or upon the acquisition or security of any property of whatsoever nature and wheresoever situate to the intent that my Trustees shall have the same full and unrestricted power of investing in all respects as if they were absolutely entitled thereto beneficially- *(Not necessary if STEP provisions are used)*

POWER TO INSURE

MY TRUSTEES may insure any trust property (including property to which someone is absolutely entitled) for any amount (including an amount which allows for increases in costs and expenses through inflation or otherwise) against any risks (including the risk of any kind of consequential loss and the risk of public or third part liability) and may pay the premiums out of the income or the capital of the property insured or any other property held on the same trust-*(Not necessary if STEP provisions are used)*

I DECLARE that all income received after my death shall be treated and applied as income from whatever source or class of investment or property the same shall arise and even if the property in respect of which the income arises is sold for the payment of my debts or for other purposes and whatever the period may be in respect of which the income shall have accrued and that no property not actually producing income shall be treated as producing income-

CHARGING CLAUSE FOR PROFESSIONAL EXECUTORS

ANY TRUSTEE being a person engaged in a profession or business may act and be paid for all work done and time expended by himself or his firm in like manner as if he not having been appointed a Trustee hereof had been employed by the Trustees to do such work including acts of business which a Trustee not being engaged in such profession or business could have done personally-*(Not necessary if STEP provisions are used)*

Attestation clause

IN WITNESS whereof I have hereunto set my hand this   day of   Two Thousand ^^^^

SIGNED by the said ^^^^^^ the Testator/Testatrix as and for his/her last Will and testament in the presence of us both being present at the same time who at his/her request in his/her presence and in the presence of each other have hereunto subscribed our name as witnesses-

SIGNED by the above named ^^^^^^ in our joint presence and then by us in his-

SIGNED by the above named ^^^^ in our joint presence and then by us in hers-

SIGNED by the said ^^^^^ the Testatrix and as for her last Will and testament in the presence of us both present at the same time who at her request in her presence and in the presence of each other have hereunto subscribed our names as witnesses-

<u>CODICILS</u>

For Codicils……..

IN all other respects I confirm my said Will

IN WITNESS whereof I have hereunto set my hand this   day of   Two Thousand and ^^^^^^

SIGNED by the said   ^^^^^^^^^^^^^^^^^^^^^^^^^^^^^^^^^^^^^
)
As a Codicil to her Will in the joint presence of us both   )
Present at the same time who at her request in her   )
presence and in the presence of each other have   )
hereunto subscribed our names as witnesses-   )

TRUSTS

This is an area of law which can confuse the man in the street as it is a term that is used but not fully understood. It is in effect a legal device by which assets may be held on behalf of another.

The most basic trust is when a person under 18 who cannot give a valid receipt has assets held on his or her behalf until they reach the age of majority. Before the age of 18 the assets will be held by trustees and during that time the assets will be held on trust.

TRUSTEES

These are the people who have control of the property and take responsibility for the running of the trust.

BENEFICIARIES

These are the people who have the benefit of the trusts

WHY A TRUST SHOULD BE CREATED

➢ They are used for a variety of purposes

➢ To preserve assets which people retain in the family from being dissipated.

➢ As previously mentioned for land and other property to be held on behalf of a child who is incapable of holding such property in their own right. This arises because a minor cannot give a valid receipt for property.

➢ To create a pension fund
➢ To operate investments on behalf of others such as unit trusts
➢ As a tax saving device.

The situations where a trust might arise are as follows

Children

If you wish to make a gift to a child then a trust is necessary for legal reasons.

LIFE INTERESTS

If the testator wishes to leave property to another to be held by them during their lifetime and thereafter to another.

This would arise if say on a second marriage the testator wanted to allow his wife to reside in the matrimonial home and once she died the property to go to his children. The wife would be what is known as the life tenant and has the right to occupy the property during her life time. The wife therefore merely has the life interest and the property is held on trust for both her and the children

CONTINGENT INTERESTS

This is when a gift is given on a condition or contingent basis. The most common example is when a gift is made to someone until they achieve a certain age such as 21 or 25.

If a gift is given immediately is known as vested. When there is a condition it is contingent that is awaiting the passing of some event on this occasion the age of 21 or 25.

DIFFERENT TYPES OF TRUSTS
THE DISCRETIONARY TRUST

This can be used for tax planning purposes. It gives the trustees the right that is the discretion to deal with the property in the trust as they see fit.

THE ACCUMULATION AND MAINTENANCE TRUST

These are used for the benefit of children and grandchildren

THE INTEREST IN POSSESSION TRUST

This is where the beneficiaries have the right to use the property.

WHAT CAN THE TRUSTEES DO?

The trustees' powers come from a variety of sources being from the trust deed itself. Statutory authority and common law authority.

Appropriation

➤ Apportionment

➤ Investment

➤ Maintenance of a child

➤ Advancement of capital

➤ The relationship between trustees and beneficiaries

➤ Trusts and saving inheritance tax

2

Enduring Powers of Attorney and Living Wills

Previously powers of attorney lapsed when the donor (that is the person giving the power) became mentally incapable. This would then involve anyone who wanted to deal the donor affairs in an application to the Court of Protection. This could be expensive and time consuming.

The other powers of attorney still exist under the Trustee Act 1925 or Powers of Attorney Act 1971. This could have the affect of terminating the appointment at the time when it might be most needed that is when the donor becomes mentally incapable.

The Enduring Powers of Attorney Act 1985 created the concept of enduring power of attorney. This means once the power has been granted that it will not be terminated on the mental incapacity of the donor.

An enduring power of attorney can be created in the following circumstances.

> ➤ The donor must be 18 that is an adult with mental capacity. They must understand the nature and extent of the power. They must understand that he attorney will be able to control the donor's affairs and continue if the donor becomes mentally incapable.

More than one attorney can be appointment. Joint attorneys can act as either jointly or severally or just jointly.

Joint means that they must act together and if one dies becomes bankrupt or loses capacity then the power ceases to exist.

Jointly and severally means that they can act independently of each. The power still exists even if the other attorney becomes incapable through bankruptcy death or incapacity

In the event of loss of mental incapacity the attorney must then register it with the Court of Protection

An enduring power of attorney may just give a specific authority to act in a certain matter. In the event of a general authority than the attorney may act in any matter that is lawful for the donor to do, otherwise the power is limited to a specific activity.

An Enduring Power of Attorney only covers legal and financial matters, it does not confer authority in respect of medical decisions

A valid EPA can only be created if the document complies with the various requirements, such as being in the form prescribed by the 1990 regulations. The form incorporates the prescribed explanatory information together with all the relevant marginal notes. It must be executed in the prescribed manner by both the donor and or the attorney. In each case in the presence of an independent witness.

Registration of the EPA with the Court of Protection

In the event of the donor becoming incapacitated mentally, the attorney is unable to act until it has been registered with the Court of Protection. This imposes special duties on the attorney which arise once the attorney has reason to believe the donor is or is becoming mentally incapable. The attorney is required to notify the donor and certain specified relatives of his intention to apply to the Court of Protection for registration. This includes husband or wife, children, parents, brothers, sisters, widow or widower and donor's grandchildren.

There is a minimum number of three who must be informed.

Effective registration re-validates the Power of Attorney and restores to the attorney the powers granted by the EPA.

Once registered the donor can no longer revoke extend or restrict the extent of the EPA.

An EPA should be given in circumstances such as when they are intending to be absent abroad, and or at the same time as making a will.

Living Wills

These are also known as advanced directives, and are intended to allow individuals to specify the nature of any medical treatment that would or not be acceptable to them in the event of their losing capacity. Although called a living will, it is not actually any form of will in the legal sense.

3

Before The Grant of Probate

Administration of the estate

This is a general term relating to the winding up of the estate. It has to be done whether there is a will and executors are appointed or if there is no will and an administrator takes over the duties of the winding up the estate. The estate is of course all the assets and liabilities of the deceased. The public tends to think of an estate as meaning only freehold land as in a landed estate. Lawyers of course mean all the deceased's worldly goods. Whether freehold leasehold or personal

Immediate steps

Registration of the death

Normally the lawyers will not be involved in the registration of the death but if you do any amount of probate you will be called upon to do it because there are no close relatives or the firm are the executors.

The responsibility of registering the death is usually upon a relative but any person present may undertake it. When the solicitor is the executor then he/ she can discharge the duty.

It must be registered in the district where the death took place or the body was found.

The death should be registered within five days but an extension can be granted.

The procedure is that the registrar will require a medical certificate of the cause of death on occasions this is sent directly to the registrar and all you need do is make an appointment.

The registrar will require details of the date and place of birth and whether or not the deceased was or had been married...

As a precaution if you hold the will make sure the names that you register are the same as the names on the will as you may have problems later on when making an application for probate.

You will have to personally check the details and sign together with paying the fee. Obtain further copies of the death certificate as necessary.

The death certificate is a certified copy of the entry of death on the register. Each copy will be £3.50 they will be more expensive later at £6.50.

Disposal of the body

It cannot be disposed off until the death has been registered and a green disposal certificate authorising whether it is a burial or cremation.

If the coroner is involved there may be delay in the registration of the death.

Any wishes by the deceased as to the disposal of the body is merely a wish and is not legally binding but most executors will respect the deceased's wishes

Funeral

It is not technically part of the executor's duties to arrange a funeral but the executor has the duty to dispose of the body. As he will be responsibility for the costs out of the estate it is usual for the executor to at least be consulted.

The direct costs of the funeral such as church, cemetery and cremation fees will be testamentary and administration expenses but not refreshments for mourners. Any payment for those out of the estate will need the permission of the residuary beneficiaries.

Burial

The funeral director makes arrangement for the burial of the body. Bodies may be buried elsewhere with permission of the local authority.

Headstones may only be erected with the permission of the priest in charge there is no automatic right to a headstone. Again the cost of the headstone will not normally be regarded as a testamentary expense. Care should be taken before disposing of all the assets of the estate that sufficient money has been held back to pay for this at a later date. An estimate will be given but a margin should be retained as it is very embarrassing at a later date to have to ask the beneficiaries to pay when they think the estate has been wound up.

Dealing with assets where no grant is required

These include

1.   Nominated property

2.   Property held on a joint tenancy: this would include land, bank accounts and building society accounts. Joint shareholdings.

3.   Life policies written in trust. Although it can be transferred immediately it does not mean that it will not be subject to Inheritance tax if it comes within the tax limit.

Obtaining the will

Solicitors and banks will only normally produce the Will on production of the death certificate and authority from the executors.

Care should be taken that it is the last Will.

With the executors instructions you should send copies of the Will to the residuary beneficiaries.

Taking possession of the deceased persons estate

You should take possession of anything of a financial nature relating the deceased's estate which ranges from actual cash to title deeds.

It is good practice when receiving items from the relatives to produce a comprehensive checklist. Send a copy of the schedule to the relatives as soon as possible. This will form the basis of the estate account. Also it will resolve any future problems as you can quite rightly claim that you only have possession of the items that are on the checklist. Try not to take possession of items that will give you problems in storing as the beneficiaries will look to you to keep them safe. Give back all bags, cases etc as otherwise your office will end up looking like a left luggage office and you will never know if ever when or how to dispose of these items. They may turn out to be family heirlooms. If any items are collected during the administration be absolutely scrupulous about asking for receipts before they leave your possession. If in doubt about anyone's authority or identity make sure you check it before parting with the items.

These are all precautions to keep down any potential complaints.

There is circumstance when assets may turn up later and an amended account can be submitted to the Inland Revenue. You should impress on the executors / administrators their duty to give a full and frank disclosure of the estate to the Inland Revenue, similarly with their duty to the beneficiaries.

The more detailed and evidential your account the less likely you are to have an enquiry from the revenue if all values are backed up by professional and current valuations your clients will have discharged their duties to the best of their abilities.

Practical considerations

1.   secure any freehold or leasehold property. Obtain keys arrange for them to be locked etc.

2.   disconnection or inform utilities such as water gas electricity.

3.   all deliveries have been stopped or post-redirected.

Insurance

Check there is an insurance policy in existence and contact insurance company about the interim arrangements.

Powers of Personal representatives before the grant

Executors

An executor's powers come from the death and the Will. The grant of probate is merely a confirmation to those powers. In reality the power is restricted by the fact that any other parties holding the assets will not release the money until a grant of probate has been produced.

Administrators

Their powers derive from the grant of administration, therefore they do not have the powers of an executor.

It is important that the administrator does not intermeddle with the estate as otherwise he will not be able to renounce afterwards.

Certain basic activities such as insuring the property and feeding animals would be regarded as necessary and not intermeddling.

<u>Vesting</u>

Property vests in the executor immediately but not with the administrator.

Obviously on the sale of property such as land the purchaser will expect to see the grant of probate even though it automatically vests in the executor.

Ascertaining the assets and liabilities.

<u>Good practice is to use a checklist and examples as follows:</u>

1.   Will

Where kept

Letter of Authority to release

Name & Address of Executors

1) ....   2).............................

....

....

.

3) ....   4).............................

....

.

....

1.   No Will

Entitlement to estate...

Name & Address of Administrators

1)

....

....

....

2.   Particulars of Deceased

Full Name..

Alias..

Date of Death   ....   Dateof Birth..............

Last Usual Address...

Married Status: Married / Single / Divorced / Widowed

Occupation...

Surviving Relatives:

Spouse [] Children   [   ] Parents [   ]

Domicile:

England & Wales   [   ] Scotland   [   ]

Wales   [   ]

National Insurance

Number...

45

Accountant:

Name...

Address..

Stockbroker / Financial Advisor

Name...

Address..

Bank Details

Name   ....   Account no.........

Address..

Joint Property

Asset:

House   [   ] Bank a/c [   ] Investments [   ]

Description...

Joint Holder...

Joint Tenants   [   ]   Tenants in Common   [

Schedule of assets and debts

Asset	Probate Value £	Corrected Value £	Grant Registered	Proceeds £
Stocks Shares				
National Savings Certificates				
Building Society a/c				
Current a/c Bank				
Deposit a/c Bank				
Premium Bonds				
Life Policies Bonds				
Freehold Property				
Leasehold Property				

Debts

Creditor Name	Nature of Debt	Amount £	Corrected Amount £	Date Paid
Utilities				
Inland Revenue				
Funeral A/c				

This checklist can immediately form the basis of the estate account and can be split into assets and liabilities.

VALUING THE ESTATE

Letters should be sent to all holders of assets that need valuation

The letter should ask

1.   Details of the asset i.e. how much is in the account.

2.   Any income that has accrued since death such as interest.

3.   Send a copy of the death certificate as banks will normally expect to see this.

4.   Ask for any forms which may become necessary to sell or close the account for signature by the executors after the grant of probate.

Bank and building society accounts

You will need to ask the following

1.   Balance plus interest if any

2.   Details of any other accounts

3.   Any items held on safe deposit.

4.   Details of any standing orders or any money received after date of death which may need to be refunded such as pension payments.

5.   You may need to borrow the IHT liability so ask them for any details that they might want.

Banks and building societies are more liberal about this and it is better to ask for money in the existing account if this is possible. If not a loan will need to be set up.

Stocks and shares

A list of all the shares should be set up.

You need to be meticulous with the actual share certificates that you take possession of. Make sure you create a schedule and get the executors or informants to sign the list by way of confirmation that is all they have given you.

People are exceedingly lax with certificates. And arguments can arise later as to what originals you possess

Obtain valuation from a stockbroker for which a fee is payable. Take instructions from the beneficiaries if at some date they wish them to be sold.

National Savings

Make application to the Director of Savings to obtain a valuation and forms to cash the holdings if necessary.

Building society accounts

Similar letter as to bank.

Social security /Pension

Letter to local office ask for balances or amounts owed.

Private Pension scheme

As above

Life Assurance

Obtain value of policy

Obtain Claim form

Land

An estate agent's valuation. Unless it is a farm then a full professional valuation as you may be claiming a relief.

It is possible for the executors to give a valuation but the district valuer will be keen to be involved. Also you need to be aware that for Capital Gains Tax purposes that the value at death will be the start value for the beneficiaries if the property is sold at a later date or transferred by way of assent. It is therefore important to get this right even if no IHT is payable. It will be much more difficult many years later to do a back calculation. Remind beneficiaries of this so that you are not involved in hours of abortive work at some future date.

Funeral expenses

It is good practice to ask the holders of any funds to pay the funeral account. This has a double effect. It removes any embarrassment by the beneficiaries as the funeral director may contact them. It helps the funeral directors cash flow and cuts down any further administration by you.

Council Tax

There will be an exemption so write to the council immediately if the property is empty.

All other debts

Write and ask for accounts and state you will pay them once probate has been granted and the funds are available.

Inland Revenue

If the deceased had an accountant supply him with a copy of death certificate and ask for his requirements.

Statutory advertisements

By advertising a personal representative will discharge his duty for payment of accounts not known by him.

Searches

Should you do a bankruptcy search against the deceased? Similarly you may wish to take a bankruptcy search against any large beneficiaries as if you pay them the money and not their trustee in bankruptcy you may not have discharged your duty.

The Executors may be liable if property / money is handed to someone who is bankrupt. They cannot give a valid receipt

Taxation of the Estate

There are three taxes that could affect the estate.

1. Income Tax
2. Capital Gains Tax
3. Inheritance Tax

The personal representatives are under a duty to deal with the deceased's tax affairs, and settle any outstanding liabilities and claim any rebates that may be necessary.

If the estate is large enough they will have to complete and submit the Inheritance Tax Account before probate or Letters of Administration will be granted.

In the event of inheritance tax having to be paid this will have to be paid before the grant is made.

Income tax

A return must be made to the Inland Revenue with the deceased's income up to the date of the death. The personal representative therefore should write to the Inland Revenue, firstly to report the death and secondly to obtain a return to discover whether any tax may be due or owed to the estate.

The estate is entitled to the full personal reliefs for the tax year in question regarding the death.

Income received

Income received during the administration period.

There may be income that is being received during the administration period, such as salary, rent, dividends and interest on any investments.

Estate Income

This is income received during the administration period and finishes on the day when the value of the residuary estate is calculated for distribution purposes.

The personal representative must pay income tax received during the administration period although there are no personal reliefs.

The only advantage is that the estate in not liable for a higher rate tax which is currently 40%. There is relief for any interest paid, and may arise as a result of obtaining allowance for the inheritance tax.

Capital Gains Tax

The personal representatives must settle any Capital gains tax payable on any gains made during the deceased's lifetime. There is no Capital gains tax liability just as a result of the death and the personal representatives and beneficiaries ultimately are treated as acquiring the assets on the deceased's death, at their market value at the date of death.

It can therefore be very important to have a correct valuation of assets even though inheritance tax may not be payable, this will be the starting point for the beneficiaries in any future capital gains tax liability.

Inheritance Tax

Inheritance tax is payable on the value of all the property that the deceased owned, up to the date of death. This includes property passing under his will, or under the intestacy rules as well as property held under a joint tenancy and nominated property. There are important exemptions, depending on who is the beneficiary, and no inheritance tax will be payable in the following circumstances.

- Spouse of a deceased
- A Charity
- A Political party
- Some national bodies such as museums and art galleries

Inheritance tax may be avoided is there is business property or agricultural property relief and inheritance tax may be payable if the deceased has died within seven years of making a lifetime gift. There is however tapering relief over the seven year period.

Raising funds for paying the IHT on the personality

It is possible to pay instalments on land but not on the personal possessions. This has to be paid before the grant is made so you may have to borrow the tax before you have access to the funds.

Once borrowed or accessed the cheque will usually be in favour of the Inland Revenue.

Building Societies

This could be your best source of funds as they may allow you to have a cheque with only forms signed by the executors.

Direct Payment Scheme

Banks are now more susceptible to paying the money direct to the Inland Revenue which is only fair as it is the deceased's money and therefore the estates.

Beneficiary

Some beneficiaries may be able to pay IHT out of their own resources so as not to incur interest. Please ask.

4

AFTER THE GRANT

The grant of representation is the official document issued by the court and is conclusive proof that the administrators or executors legal authority to deal with the estate.

Registration

When making an application for probate you need to state how many office copies you require. At forty pounds for the Grant and one pound each sealed office copy you should obtain enough for you to send copies to collect in the estate expeditiously.

It is good practice to send a photocopy to the executors/ beneficiaries to prove you have probate. Make it clear it is not an office copy as otherwise they will start using it for their own purposes and will be very disappointed when they get turned down by banks etc.

Whilst registering the grant you should send any claim form along so as to transfer withdraw or sell the assets. These should have been signed in readiness by the executors.

Deposit

As money comes in over and above what you need to settle immediate debts you should be putting the funds on deposit. If in a separate interest bearing account this will assist as you will not have to calculate the interest payable if it has been on deposit throughout the administration.

Realising the Assets

The most urgent matter may be paying off the IHT loan

Clearing the tax liabilities

Complete the tax return form R27 or R40
You should complete the tax return form for the period from the previous 6 April to the date of death.

Clearing the IHT position

The personal representatives may have given their own estimate of the value. As previously mentioned this value could have an effect on future tax for the beneficiaries Capital gains tax purposes. If the property is well below the IHT limit then the value of the land should be put in at as high a valuation as possible.

If the property that is subject to IHT is sold later for a lower figure than the probate value agreed then, if within three years of the date of death, you will be able to claim IHT loss relief.

Payment on account

If you have elected to pay by instalments, the instalment within six months after the end of the month on which the death occurred any tax outstanding is subject to interest.

Corrective account

If there is any variation on the agreed figures after the estate has been settled then a corrective account can be submitted for an overpayment or underpayment. If only minor then it may be acceptable to do this by letter and an assessment will be issued.

Clearance certificate.

Once all IHT has been paid and before final distribution you should obtain a clearance certificate form the capital taxes Offices on an IHT30. This will give the personal perspectives protection against any further claims.

If further assets become available obviously they should be declared

Instalment Option - Property

The personal representatives may elect to pay tax by instalments of up to ten equal instalments per year over ten years on land, certain securities and businesses.

Capital Gains tax

No charge to capital Gains tax arises on death. The assets are deemed to have been acquired at their market value at that date.

When the asset is transferred to the beneficiaries they are deemed to have acquired the assets at the value at death.

If there is a chargeable gain during the administration after claiming their allowances it will be subject to 40 per cent tax.

Inland Revenue Charge

Whilst there is tax outstanding the Inland Revenue have a charge against those assets.

DISTRIBUTION OF THE ESTATE

EXECUTOR'S YEAR

Personal representatives have a year from the date of death before the beneficiaries can call upon them to distribute any part of the estate this is called the executors' year.

Personal representatives should protect themselves before distributing the estate.

The problems that could arise are an Outstanding tax liabilities this could include IHT, CGT and Income Tax. Obtain clearance certificates for all those:

Outstanding Debts

Place statutory advert if in doubt. Ones to look out for are funeral expenses and the headstone which may be placed later.

Unknown beneficiaries

Such as all the grandchildren these include both legitimate and illegitimate relatives.

Rectification action

There is a possibility that the will might be rectified within the first six months. Any action after six months requires leave of the court and the personal representatives are protected.

Family provision claims

Again if within the six months there may be a family provision claim.

Variation or disclaimer

Any deed of family arrangement could mean that a beneficiary will not accept a gift and disclaimer cannot be made once a beneficiary has accepted the gift.

Specific Problems - Dead Beneficiaries

If a beneficiary has died before the testator prima facie the gift will lapse unless the gift was of the whole or part of the residue in which case it will pass on to the person's estate.

Bankrupt beneficiaries.

It might be good practice to search against the beneficiaries as if any gift should be paid to the trustee in bankruptcy, the personal representatives need a valid receipt.

Which property pays the tax?

The Will should provide this

Specific Gift

This will entitle the beneficiary to all income and interest on that item since death it still does not become the property of the beneficiary until it has been vested in them

Assents of land.

This transfers the land to the beneficiaries. Now an AS1

Although no stamp duty you still have to complete an SDLT form.

Memorandum of the assent should be endorsed on the probate. This is obviously not so important now that land is registered as it would be difficult to try and transfer the same piece of land twice without becoming immediately aware of it!

FORMALITIES TO TRANSFER VARIOUS ASSETS

Personal chattels etc

By delivery no set method may be by conduct writing or verbally.

Bank account

Written instructions to bank or by cheque to beneficiary

National savings certificate etc

Withdrawal forms

Stocks and shares

Share or stock transfer forms.

Registered/Unregistered land

AS1

Schedule of Probate Forms

1. 1HT205 - Return of estate Information
2. 1HT200- Inland Revenue Account for Inheritance Tax
3. 1HTWS- Inheritance Tax Work Sheet
4. Oath for Executors
5. Oath for Administrators
6. Stock/Share Transfer Form
7. AS1

The following Probate forms, which are shown overleaf, are obtainable on the website:

www.Hmcourt-service.gov-uk .

Also: www.probate.co.uk/advice

8. N205D-Notice of Issue (Probate Claim)
9. PA1-How to Obtain probate
10. PA1A-Guidance notes for Probate Application
11. PA1S-Application for Probate search
12. PA2-How to Obtain probate-Guide for the Applicant Without Solicitor
13. PA3-Probate Fees
14. PA4 Director of Probate Registries and Interview venues
15. PA6-My probate Appointment-What Happens next?

Notice of issue
(probate claim)

In the

Claim No.

Claimant(s)

Defendant(s)

Issue fee

In the estate of   deceased (Probate)

Your claim was issued on [   ]

[The court sent it to the defendant(s) by first class post on [   ]

and it will be deemed served on [   ]].

[The claim form (which includes particulars of claim) is returned to you, with the relevant response forms, for

you to serve them on the defendant(s)]

Notes for guidance

The claim form and particulars of claim, if served separately, must be served on the defendant within 4 months of the date of issue (6 months if you are serving outside England and Wales). You may be able to apply to extend the time for serving the claim form but the application must generally be made before the 4 month or 6 month period expires.

You must inform the court immediately if your claim is settled.

The defendant must file an acknowledgment of service and defence within 28 days of service of the Particulars of Claim (whether they are served with the claim form or separately). A longer period applies if the defendant is served outside England and Wales.

Default judgment **cannot** be obtained in a probate claim.

If no defendant acknowledges service or files a defence, and the time for doing so has expired, you may apply to the court for an order that the claim proceed to trial.

To

Ref.

N205D Notice of issue (probate) (10.01)

Probate Application Form - PA1

Please use **BLOCK CAPITALS**

Name of deceased

Forenames
Surname

Please state where you wish to be interviewed (see enclosed PA4). You can be interviewed at the Controlling Probate Registry of your choice or at one of its interview venues. Please also specify dates when you will **not** be available for interview.

Please read the following questions and PA2 booklet 'How to obtain probate' carefully before filling in this form. Please also refer to the Guidance Notes enclosed where an item is marked *.

		Section A: The Will / Codicil	This column is for official use

*A1 Did the deceased leave a will/codicil? (Note: These may not necessarily be formal documents. If the answer to question 1 is Yes, you must enclose the **original** document(s) with your application.)

	Will		Codicil	
Yes ☐	No ☐	Yes ☐	No ☐

If **No** to both questions, please go to Section B

Date of will/codicil

A2 Is there anyone under 18 years old who receives anything in the will/codicil?

Yes ☐   No ☐

A3 Are there any executors named in the will/codicil?

Yes ☐   No ☐

*A4 Give the names of those executors who are **not** applying and the reasons why. Please see attached Guidance Notes. **All** executors **must** be accounted for.

Full names	Reason A,B,C,D,E

A = Pre-deceased
B = Died after the deceased
C = Power Reserved
D = Renunciation
E = Power of Attorney

*B1 - B6

Please refer to the Guidance Notes

	Section B: Relatives of the deceased		

Please state the **number** of relatives in **each** category and complete each category fully (i.e. B1, B2 etc.).

If there are no relatives in a particular category, write 'nil' in each box and move onto the next category.

Number (if none, write nil)	Under 18	Over 18
B1 Surviving **lawful** husband or wife		
B2a Sons or daughters who survived the deceased		
b Sons or daughters who did **not** survive the deceased		
c Children of person(s) indicated at '2b' **only** who survived the deceased *		
B3 Parents who survived the deceased		
B4a Brothers or sisters who survived the deceased		
b Brothers or sisters who did **not** survive the deceased		
c Children of person(s) indicated at '4b' **only** who survived the deceased *		
B5 Grandparents who survived the deceased		
B6a Uncles or aunts who survived the deceased		
b Uncles or aunts who did **not** survive the deceased		
c Children of person(s) indicated at '6b' **only** who survived the deceased *		

Section C: Details of applicant(s)

Please note that the grant will normally be sent to the first applicant. Any applicant named will be required to attend an interview. It is, however, usually only necessary for one person to apply (please see PA2 booklet, page 3).

I.T.W.C

C1   Title

Mr ☐   Mrs ☐   Miss ☐   Ms ☐   Other ☐

C2   Forenames

C3   Surname

C4   Address

Postcode: _____

C5   Telephone number

Home _____

Work _____

C6   Occupation

C7   Are you related to the deceased?

Yes ☐   No ☐

If Yes, what is your relationship?

Relationship: _____

C8   If there are any other applicants, up to a maximum of three, give their details. (Note: **All** applicants named in Sections C1 and C8 must attend an interview.)

Details of other applicants who wish to be named in the grant of representation. (Please give details as C1 to C7.)

C9   Name and address of any surviving lawful husband or wife of the deceased, unless stated above.

Postcode: _____

*C10   If you are applying as an attorney on behalf of the person entitled to the grant, please state their name, address and capacity in which they are entitled (e.g. relationship to the deceased).

Postcode: _____

Relationship: _____

C10a   Has the person named in section C10 signed an Enduring Power of Attorney?

Yes ☐   No ☐

C10b   If Yes, has it been registered with the Public Guardianship Office?

Yes ☐   No ☐

			This column is for official use
	Section D: Details of the deceased		
*D1	Forenames		
*D2	Surname		True name
*D3	Did the deceased hold any assets (excluding joint assets) in another name?	Yes ☐ No ☐	Alias
*D4	If Yes, what are the assets?		
	And in what name(s) are they held?		
D5	Last permanent address of the deceased.		Address
		Postcode:	
D6	Date of birth		
D7	Date of death	Age:	D/C district and No.
D8	Was England and Wales the permanent home of the deceased? If No, please specify the deceased's permanent home.	Yes ☐ No ☐	L.S.A. D.B.F.

*D9   Tick the last **legal** marital status of the deceased, and give dates where appropriate.

Bachelor/Spinster ☐

Widowed ☐

Married ☐   Date:

Divorced ☐   Date:

Note: These documents (✦) may usually be obtained from the Court which processed the divorce/separation.

*(If the deceased did **not** leave a will, please enclose official copy✦ of the Decree Absolute.)*

Judicially separated ☐   Date:

*(If the deceased did **not** leave a will, please enclose official copy✦ of the Decree of Judicial Separation.)*

*D10   Was the deceased legally adopted?   Yes ☐   No ☐

*D11   Has any relative of the deceased been legally adopted?   Yes ☐   No ☐

(If Yes, give name and relationship to deceased.)

Name:

Relationship:

D12   *Answer this section **only** if the deceased died **before 4th April 1988** or left a will or codicil dated before that date.*

D12a   Was the deceased illegitimate?   Yes ☐   No ☐

D12b   Did the deceased leave any illegitimate sons or daughters?   Yes ☐   No ☐

D12c   Did the deceased have any illegitimate sons or daughters who died leaving children of their own?   Yes ☐   No ☐

Important - please complete the checklist overleaf before submitting your application

Checklist

Important

Please return your forms to the probate registry which controls the interview venue at which you wish to be interviewed (see PA4) otherwise your application may be delayed.

Before sending your application, please complete this checklist to confirm that you have enclosed the following items:

1   PA1 (Probate Application Form) ☐

2   Either IHT205 (signed by all applicants) ☐
     or D18 (signed) ☐
     Note: Do not enclose IHT Form 200 – **this must be sent to C.T.O.** (see PA2)

3   Original will and codicil(s), **not a photocopy** ☐
     Note: Do **not** attach anything to the will/codicil

4   Official copy of death certificate or coroner's letter, **not a photocopy** ☐

5   Other documents as requested on PA1 – please specify

6   Please state number of official copy grants required for use in England and ☐
     Wales (see PA3)

7   Please state number of official copy grants required for use **outside** ☐   **For official use only**
     England and Wales (see PA3)   **(sealed and certified)**

8   Please state total amount of cheque enclosed for fee   £
     (made payable to HMCS) including cost for the number of official
     copy grants stated in 6 and 7 above.

Note: If you do not enclose all the relevant items, your application may be delayed.

Official Use Only

Type of grant:

Power reserved to _____ [Name of executor/s]

Will message: with a codicil / and _____ codicils (delete as appropriate)

Limitation _____

Min interest   Yes / No

Life interest   Yes / No

Figures:- DNE / amounts to Gross: £
                       Net: £   Fee paid: £

Clearing:-

Title:-

Footnote:-

Application for a probate search

www.theprobateservice.gov.uk

When completing your form please use CAPITAL LETTERS

Details of the Deceased

Surname

Forenames

Probate details (if known)

Grant type: Issuing Registry: Grant issue date:

Date of death/search period*

Address

* (see Conditions of Service on next page)

Document requirements/payment

Do you want a copy of the Will (if any)?   Yes ☐   No ☐   If Yes, how many? ☐

Do you want a copy of the Grant of Probate or Letters of Administration (if any)?   Yes ☐   No ☐   If Yes, how many? ☐

I enclose a crossed cheque/Postal Order (payable to HM Courts Service) to the value of   (see notes on fees on next page)   £

Your own details

Name/Organisation

Your ref. (if any)

Address/DX number and Exchange

Please send the completed form, together with your payment, by post to: The Postal Searches and Copies Department, The Probate Registry, Castle Chambers, Clifford Street, York YO1 9RG (DX720629 York 21)

For official use

Postal Searches and Copies Department:
Information and Conditions of Service

Applicable dates and records held: The Postal Searches and Copies Department has indexes relating to all Probate records for the whole of England and Wales from 11 January 1858 up to the present day. You may apply for a copy of any proved Will, as well as a copy of the Grant of Representation. The Grant will tell you who were the Executors or Administrators (those appointed to gather in and distribute the estate). It may also tell you the name of the Solicitor acting for them (if any) and the value of the estate, although usually only in very broad terms. The financial summary shown on the Grant is unfortunately the only information relating to the estate that the Probate record contains. No inventory or estate accounts are available. Occasionally, further details are available from the Capital Taxes Office, but you will normally need the written consent of the executors or administrators. **Please note that, if Probate has not been granted, the Probate Service will have no record of the estate and will therefore not be able to provide copies of any document relating to it.**

If the death was recent, it may be that Probate has not yet been cleared. The Probate procedure itself normally takes some weeks, and there may have been a considerable further delay before the application for Probate was made. Consequently, it may be advisable to wait two or three months after the date of death before having a search made, in order to allow time for the Probate process to be completed.

If you apply before Probate has been completed, you will be notified that no details are available. If you wish to pursue your enquiry, you will need to reapply after a suitable interval, enclosing a further fee and resubmitting all the relevant details, or enter a Standing Search. A Standing Search remains in force for a period of 6 months from the date of entry and provides copies of the Will (if any) and Grant if a Grant issues during this period. Contact the Postal Searches and Copies Department or any Probate Registry for further details.

Other parts of the UK and the Republic of Ireland: The jurisdiction of the Probate Service is limited to England and Wales. If the deceased died domiciled in Scotland, you could try contacting HM Commissary Office, 27 Chambers Street, Edinburgh EH1 2NS (Tel: 0131 247 2850) if the death occurred after 1985, or the Scottish Records Office, HM General Register House, Edinburgh EH1 3YY (Tel: 0131 535 1334) for records prior to this. For Northern Ireland, contact the Probate and Matrimonial Office, The Royal Courts of Justice, Belfast BT1 3JF (Tel: 028 9023 5111), or, if the death occurred more than 7 years ago, the Public Record Office of Northern Ireland, 66 Balmoral Street, Belfast, BT9 6NY (Tel: 028 9025 1318). For the Republic of Ireland, contact the Probate Office, Fourt Courts, Dublin 7 (Tel: Dublin 725555), or the National Archives Office, Bishop Street, Dublin 8 (Tel: Dublin 407 2300) for records more than 20 years old. The Channel Islands and the Isle of Man also have independent Probate Courts.

Fees: When returning the completed application to the Postal Searches and Copies Department in York, please also enclose the fee of £5.00. Each **extra copy** of the same document ordered at the same time will attract an additional fee of £1.00. Cheques or Postal Orders should be crossed and made payable to 'HM Courts Service'. Fees from abroad should be paid by International Money Order, cheque or draft, payable through a United Kingdom bank, and must be made out in £ sterling. We are currently unable to accept payments by credit or debit card, nor are we able to receive search requests by telephone. Please contact the Postal Searches and Copies Department for details of fees for special copies (for instance if you are administering estate abroad), and mark your application accordingly.

The standard fee covers a 4-year search starting from the year in which the death occurred (or the year from which you ask us to start searching). Longer searches are charged at a rate of £3.00 per 4-year period, so that an 8-year search will cost £8.00, and a 12-year search £11.00. Please specify the period to be searched (as well as the date of death if known) and send the appropriate fee. If the death occurred within the last 4 years, the search will be made up to the most recent index. If the search is successful, we will obtain and forward copies of the Will and/or Grant as requested. If no Grant has issued in this time, you will be notified accordingly. We aim to respond to your request within 21 working days.

If a record is traced, the standard fee includes one copy of the Will, if any, and Grant, if requested. Please state clearly which document(s) you require. If the details you supply are incomplete, ambiguous or incorrect and the documents cannot be traced as a result, you will be asked to reapply, giving the correct information and enclosing a further payment. We cannot accept responsibility for the accuracy of the search unless full and correct details are given that accord with the information supplied on application for the Grant, normally the information in the Register of Deaths. If there is insufficient information to make a search, we will contact you for further details. **Please note that your payment is not refundable in the event of a negative search result.**

Original documents: If you are applying for copies of older documents, you should be aware that some of these are in poor condition. Although we make every effort to produce a legible copy from the documents we hold, a small proportion will be of unavoidable poor quality. Furthermore, copies are normally made from the record copies held by the Probate Service. This means that documents prior to the early 1930s will be, by default, copies of manuscript or typescript record copies, and not facsimile copies of the original document. If you want facsimile copies of the original, you will need to mark your request very clearly to that effect.

Guidance Notes
for Probate Application Form PA1

These notes will help you to complete the parts of form PA1 marked *

A1 Please enclose the original will and any codicils with your application (**not** a photocopy).

A4 Please state the names of any executors named in the will who are not applying for the Grant of Probate and show one of the following reasons for this:-

A The executor died before the deceased.

B The executor died after the deceased.

C The executor does not wish to apply for probate now but wishes to reserve the right to act as executor in the future if necessary – this option is referred to as having "power reserved".

D The executor does not wish to apply for probate at all. This is referred to as "renouncing". It means that he / she gives up all his/her rights to act as executor.

E The executor wants to appoint another person to act as his / her attorney to take the Grant of Representation out on his / her behalf. Please note, however, that the attorney of one executor cannot take a grant jointly with an executor acting in his own right.

If you give reason D or E, please send a letter signed by the executor stating their intention when you send the application to the Probate Registry. If option C, D, or E is stated the Probate Registry will, on receipt of your application, send you a form for the executor(s) to sign to confirm their intention. You should arrange for this to be completed and then return it to the Probate Registry as instructed.

Example for A4:

A will appoints three executors – Brian Jones, Valerie Jones and Frank Smith. Brian Jones wishes to apply for the grant, Frank Smith dies before the deceased and Valerie Jones does not wish to apply for the grant at present, as she works full time and cannot attend the appointment. Valerie wishes to keep her options open however, just in case it becomes necessary for her to take out a Grant of Probate in future e.g. if Brian Jones dies before he has completed the administration. The form would be completed as follows:

| Frank Smith | A |
| Valerie Jones | C |

The Grant of Probate will issue to Brian Jones with "power reserved" to Valerie Jones. Valerie Jones will be asked to sign a "power reserved" form.

Please complete the **whole** of Section B

Note:

■ This section refers to blood relatives only; details of step relatives are not required.

■ The term "survived" means the person was alive when the deceased died.

■ If the deceased had any half brothers or sisters / uncles / aunts (i.e. only one parent in common), please indicate this on the form.

B2(c), B4(c), and B6(c)

B2(c) – Do **not** include children of sons / daughters of the deceased who survived the deceased.

B4(c) – Do **not** include children of brothers / sisters of the deceased who survived the deceased.

B6(c) – Do **not** include children of aunts / uncles of the deceased who survived the deceased.

Section C

C10

If you are applying on behalf of the person entitled to the grant (i.e. as their attorney), you should send a letter signed by them confirming that they want you to apply with your application. If the person entitled to the grant has already signed an Enduring Power of Attorney, please send the original document to us.

Section D

D1 - D2

Please state the full **true** name of the deceased. The true name consists of the forenames as shown on the person's birth certificate and the surname as shown on the death certificate.

D3 - D4

If the deceased had any assets in any name(s) other than his / her true name these should be stated. You do not need to show here any assets held jointly with another person.

Example for D1 - D4:

Name on birth certificate	Emma Louise **Jones**
Name on death certificate	Emma Louise **Smith**

The deceased's true name is Emma Louise Smith.

The deceased had a bank account in the name of Louise Smith and was commonly known by this name. The form should be completed as follows:

Forenames	**Emma Louise**
Surname	Smith
Did the deceased hold any assets (excluding joint assets) in another name?	Yes
If yes, what are the assets?	Lloyds Bank Account
And in what name(s) are they held?	**Louise** Smith

The grant will issue in the name of "Emma Louise Smith otherwise known as Louise Smith".

D9 You do not need to supply a copy of the Decree Absolute or decree of Judicial Separation if the deceased left a will.

D10 - D11

If the deceased did **not** leave a will and the applicant for the grant is the adoptor/adoptee of the deceased, please file a copy of the entry in the Adopted Children's Register. An official copy of the entry in the Adopted Children's Register can be obtained from The General Register Office, Adoption Section, Smedley Hydro, Trafalgar Road, Birkdale, Southport PR8 2HH.

**If you have any general enquiries, please telephone
the Probate and Inheritance Tax Helpline
Telephone number: 0845 3020900 (calls to this number are charged at local rate)**

 **HER MAJESTY'S COURTS SERVICE hmcs**

How to obtain probate - A guide for the applicant acting without a solicitor

If you make a personal application for a Grant of Probate you will be required to attend an appointment at one of our interview venues.

Important

Please read through this booklet carefully before you start to complete the enclosed application forms. The following information will help you decide whether you need probate and to fill in the forms if you do. It should answer most of your queries about probate. If you have any difficulties completing the forms or need further guidance please contact your local Probate Registry. The staff are there to help you – but they are unable to give you legal advice. Applying for probate yourself is a fairly straightforward procedure in most cases.

The information in this booklet refers only to the law in England and Wales. If the deceased was permanently resident outside England and Wales another system of law may apply – this will be explained when we receive your application.

If you need to apply for a Grant of Representation in Scotland or Northern Ireland, you should contact the court in the appropriate country.

What is Probate?

When a person dies somebody has to deal with their estate (the money property and possessions left) by collecting in all the money, paying any debts and distributing what is left to those people entitled to it. In order to get authority to do this they usually need to obtain a legal document called a **Grant of Representation** from the Probate Registry.

There are three types of Grant of Representation.

1. Probate

Issued to one or more executors named in the deceased's Will.

Note: Executors are people named in the Will to deal with the estate.

2. *Letters of Administration* (With Will)

Issued when there is a Will but there is no executor named or when the executors are unable or unwilling to apply for the grant.

3. *Letters of Administration*

Issued when the deceased has not made a Will, or any Will made is not valid.

Throughout the term **"grant"** will be used to mean whichever type of Grant of Representation you may need.

Page 1

Why is a grant necessary?

Organisations holding money in the deceased's name need to know to whom that money should be paid and the grant is proof that the person named in it may collect the money.

When a person dies the estate left passes to the people named in his or her Will. If there is no valid Will it passes to his or her next of kin.

The distribution of the estate is the responsibility of the person named in the grant.

Is a grant always needed?

Sometimes a grant is not required and you should ask anyone holding the deceased's money whether they will release it to you without seeing a grant. If they agree they may attach conditions such as asking you to sign a statutory declaration before a solicitor. It is for you to decide whether it is cheaper or easier to do this than to apply for a grant.

A grant **may** not be required in the following cases:

- If the estate is small some organisations such as insurance companies and building societies may release the money to you at their discretion.
- If the whole of the estate is held in joint names and passes automatically to the surviving joint owner. If you are in doubt on this point you may need to ask a solicitor whether a grant is needed to change the ownership of an asset.

Note: A grant will **always** be required to sell or transfer a property held in the deceased's sole name.

Important
Do not advertise any house for sale too soon after the owner's death, as a sale cannot be completed until you have obtained the grant. The date of the issue of the grant cannot be guaranteed to coincide with the final stages of any sale.

Am I entitled to a grant?

There are rules which govern who may be given a grant.

The following points are a brief guide for you:

- If there is a Will with named executors they are the first people entitled to a grant.
- If there are no executors or the executors are unable or unwilling to apply, the next person entitled to a grant is any person named in the Will to whom the estate or remainder of it, after gifts have been paid, has been given.
- If the deceased has not made a Will, application for a grant should normally be made by his or her next of kin in the following order of priority:

1. Lawful husband or wife (Note: Common-law partners have no entitlement to a grant)

2. Sons or daughters (excluding step-children)*

3. Parents

4. Brothers or sisters*

5. Grandparents

6. Uncles or aunts*.

* Or if any have died in the lifetime of the deceased then their children may apply
Note: A grant cannot be issued to any person under the age of 18.

If you are not sure whether you are entitled to apply you should still complete and return the forms and we will let you know. If you are a distant relative please supply a brief family tree showing your relationship to the deceased.

When more than one person is entitled to a grant they may all obtain a grant together. However, a maximum of four applicants is allowed and all applicants will have to attend an interview. In most cases only one person needs to obtain the grant but there are circumstances when it may be necessary for two people to do this, e.g. if anyone entitled to the estate is under the age of 18. If this is the case we will let you know as soon as possible after we have received your application.

Although the Probate Registry needs to account for all the executors named in a Will they do not all have to apply for probate. The other executor(s) may either renounce all their rights to probate or they may reserve the right to apply for probate should it become necessary in the future ("power reserved"). The "power reserved" option is the most common one and is used, for example, when the executors live in different parts of the country or it is not convenient for one of them to attend the interview due to work commitments. Only the executor(s) who attend the interview will be named on the grant and then only their signature will be required to release the assets. Please ask any executors who do not wish to apply which option they prefer and complete their details on form PA1. We will send you the relevant form for them to sign once we have checked your application.

If the person who is entitled to the grant does not wish to apply, they may appoint someone else to be their attorney to obtain the grant on their behalf. If this is the case you should complete their details on form PA1 (Section C). We will send you a form for them to sign after we receive your application.

If it is not possible to issue a grant to you, we will explain the reasons.

Will there be any tax to pay as a result of the death?

The tax on the estate of a person who has died is called **Inheritance Tax.** It is dealt with by HM Revenue and Customs (Capital Taxes). It only applies to a very small percentage of estates. If Inheritance Tax is due, you normally have to pay at least some of the tax before we can issue the grant.

The issue of the grant does not mean that HM Revenue and Customs (Capital Taxes) have agreed the final Inheritance Tax liability. They will usually contact you again after you have received the grant. Subject to the requirement to pay some of the tax before obtaining the grant, Inheritance Tax is due six months after the end of the month in which the person died. HM Revenue and Customs (Capital Taxes) will charge interest on unpaid tax from this due date whatever the reason for late payment.

Probate Registry staff are **not** trained to deal with queries about HM Revenue and Customs forms or Inheritance Tax. If you have any queries about the figures in the estate or Inheritance Tax generally, you should contact HM Revenue and Customs (Capital Taxes) Helpline on 0845 3020900. Their address is Ferrers House, PO Box 38, Castle Meadow Road, Nottingham NG2 1BB.

Note: If you are applying at Newcastle, Middlesbrough, Carlisle or York Probate Registries, you should contact the Capital Taxes helpline at Edinburgh on 0131 777 4050 or 4060. Their address is Meldrum House, 15 Drumsheugh Gardens, Edinburgh EH3 7UG.

How do I apply for a grant?

The four stages to apply for a grant are set out below:

1. Obtaining the forms

The following forms will either have been enclosed with this booklet or may be obtained from your nearest Probate Registry (see list (PA4)).

- *The Probate Application form* (PA1) and PA1a
  Forms PA1 and PA1a can also be downloaded from our website (www.theprobateservice.gov.uk). The PA1 is an interactive form and can be filled in on screen.

- The PA1 asks for details of the deceased and the applicant(s).

- *Account of the estate* (IHT205 and instruction booklet IHT206)
  IHT205 and 206 can also be downloaded from HM Revenue and Customs (Capital Taxes) website (www.hmrc.gov.uk/cto).

This form asks you to give details of the deceased's estate at the date of death. You should try to find out the full value of all items identified, including any interest or bonus which will be paid. However, reasonable estimates are acceptable and should be marked "estimated". The full market value of any house owned by the deceased should be shown although a professional valuation is not normally required. The value of household goods, jewellery and belongings should be shown as the amount for which they could be sold, not their value for insurance purposes. Please refer to the IHT206 for further guidance.

Form IHT205 is applicable in most cases but if it does not apply in your case you will need to complete a full HM Revenue and Customs Account (form IHT200). You can order this from HM Revenue and Customs (Capital Taxes) on 0845 234 1020 (answerphone service). Alternatively it can be downloaded from www.hmrc.gov.uk/ cto on the Internet. They will send you a pack including form IHT200 and form D18 (Probate Summary). In these cases you have the option of assessing any tax due yourself or asking HM Revenue and Customs (Capital Taxes) to do it for you. You should follow the instructions you receive from HM Revenue and Customs regarding IHT200 and send the completed D18 to us with your application. Do **not** send IHT200 to the Probate Registry.

If you have any queries regarding the completion of form IHT200 you should telephone HM Revenue and Customs (Capital Taxes) Helpline on 0845 3020900 or 0131 777 4050 / 4060 (see previous page).

2. Completing the forms

You should complete the relevant forms fully and tick the checklist on form PA1 to confirm that you have enclosed all the necessary paperwork and accompanying documents. Please refer to the Guidance Notes on PA1 (PA1a) and to the IHT206 booklet to assist you.

3. Returning the forms

You must send the completed forms (i.e. PA1, IHT205 or D18) together with a cheque for the fee payable - see PA3 and accompanying documents to the Probate Registry which controls the venue at which you wish to be interviewed. For a list of addresses see PA4. **Please note** – you should **not** send any correspondence to any of the local Probate interview venues as they are operated on an appointment only basis and opening times vary. You can choose to be interviewed at either a controlling Probate Registry or at one of the other interview venues.

When you return the forms PA1 and **either** IHT205 **or** D18 you should also send the following:

- An official copy of the death certificate issued by the Registrar of Births Deaths and Marriages or a Coroner's certificate. Please do **not** send a photocopy of this document.

- The **original** Will and any codicils (or any document in which the deceased expresses any wishes about the distribution of his or her estate). The original Will may be held at a solicitor's office or a bank or it may be amongst the deceased's possessions. You should make a thorough search for it and if you cannot find it you should contact your local Probate Registry. A Will may be lodged for safe-keeping at the Principal Probate Registry in London. If this is the case it will be identified when your application is examined. If you do not send the **original** Will, your application will be delayed.

We strongly advise you to make and keep a copy of any Will or codicil you send us and to send the original document(s) by recorded or guaranteed delivery together with your application forms. Please do not attach anything to the Will by staple, pin etc. or remove any fastenings from the Will.

- Any other documents specifically requested in form PA1 e.g. decree absolute.

- A cheque for the fee made payable to **HMCS** for the correct amount due (including the cost of the number of official copy grants you require). **Please refer to the fee list (PA3).**

When we receive your application we will examine it and contact you if there are any difficulties. If your application is complicated there may be additional documents to be signed or you may be asked to contact other people (for example a witness to a Will) so that we can interview them or obtain their signatures to documents to assist with your application.

If there are no problems we will, within approximately 10 working days from the date of receipt of your application, send you a letter giving you an appointment for interview at the location you have chosen. If you want us to acknowledge your application, please send a stamped addressed envelope.

4. Attending the appointment for interview

The purpose of the appointment is to confirm the details that you have given on the forms and to answer any queries you **or we** may have.

You will receive further information about the interview with your appointment letter but basically you will be asked to sign a form of oath and to swear or affirm before the interviewing officer that the information you have given is true to the best of your knowledge. The interview should last no more than ten to fifteen minutes. Each applicant will be required to bring proof of identification to the interview.

In most cases only one appointment is required.

If you are applying for a grant with someone else who is unable to attend for interview at the place you have chosen, arrangements may be made for them to attend at a different interview venue (see PA4). However this will mean that the issue of your grant will take longer.

When will I be interviewed?

No appointment can be given until your application has been examined and any queries resolved. You will then be given the earliest available date at the interview venue you have chosen. It is difficult to say how soon you will be interviewed as the number of applications waiting to be dealt with varies but, in straightforward cases, the appointment will usually take place within a month of your application being received. You will usually be able to get an earlier appointment at one of the controlling Probate Registries if required.

If we are unable to send you a notice of appointment within 10 working days of receiving your application you will normally be sent an acknowledgement of your application.

Applying for the grant when form IHT200 required

To fill in form IHT200, you should follow the guidance provided by HM Revenue and Customs (Capital Taxes). You will also need to fill in supplementary page D18 (Probate Summary). When you have finished filling in the forms, you can choose whether to work out the Inheritance Tax for yourself or you can ask HM Revenue and Customs (Capital Taxes) to do it for you. Then follow the appropriate paragraph below.

If you want HM Revenue and Customs (Capital Taxes) to work out the tax for you

When you are ready to apply for the grant, you should send form PA1, the other documents needed (see page 7) and form D18 (but **not** the form IHT200 itself) to the Probate Registry. After your interview, the form D18 will be given back to you with Section A completed. You should then send form IHT200, the supplementary pages and the form D18 to HM Revenue and Customs (Capital Taxes) who will tell you what to do next.

If you have worked out that there is some Inheritance Tax to pay

Fill in Sections B and C of form D18 by copying the details from form IHT200. Then, when you are ready to apply for the grant, you should send form PA1, the other documents needed (see page 7) and form D18 (but not the form IHT200 itself) to the Probate Registry. After your interview, form D18 will be given back to you with Section A completed. You should then send form IHT200, the relevant supplementary pages, the form D18 and your payment to HM Revenue and Customs (Capital Taxes). Provided you have paid the right amount of tax, HM Revenue and Customs (Capital Taxes) will endorse form D18 and return it direct to the Probate Registry, who will then issue the grant.

If you have worked out that there is no Inheritance Tax to pay

Fill in Sections B and C of form D18 by copying the details from form IHT200. Then, when you are ready to apply for the grant, you should send form PA1, the other documents needed (see page 7) and form D18 to the Probate Registry. At the same time, send form IHT200 and the other supplementary pages to HM Revenue and Customs (Capital Taxes). The grant will be sent to you after your interview.

How much will it cost to obtain a grant?

Please refer to the fee list (PA3).

Before submitting your application you should work out the fee payable and decide how many official copies of the grant you would like. Then send a cheque, made payable to **HMCS** for the correct amount with your application, i.e. the total of your application fee and the fee for each copy of the grant. Your application will **not** be processed until the fee has been paid.

The number of official (i.e. sealed) copies you may require will depend on how many organisations need to see the grant and how quickly you wish to deal with the estate. Unsealed photocopies of the grant are not valid and most organisations will not accept them. If there are any assets held outside England and Wales you may require a special copy of the grant – usually referred to as a sealed and certified copy. You should check this with the organisation holding the asset and order the appropriate number of copies at the time of your application.

What happens after the appointment for interview?

After your appointment the grant will be prepared by the Probate Registry and sent to you by post with any copies you have ordered.

The interviewing officer should be able to give you an estimate of how long this will take.

When you receive the grant you can show it to any person or organisation holding the deceased's money or property in order that the asset can be released, sold or transferred. You may however, be asked to provide an official copy of the grant before this can be done. If you need to order further copies of the grant after it has issued you should write to the Probate Registry which issued the grant, but please note that the copies will be more expensive than those ordered at the time of application (see PA3).

Please note that the responsibility of the Probate Registry ends when the grant is issued. We are unable to assist you in dealing with the estate after that. If you have any problems in administering the estate you should seek legal advice.

THE PROBATE SERVICE
Probate Fees

	FEE
Application In all cases where the net estate [i.e. the amount remaining in the deceased's sole name after funeral expenses and debts owing have been deducted] is <u>over £5,000</u> [see example 1 below]. **N.B. Joint assets passing automatically** to the surviving **joint owner should not be included when calculating the fee.**	£90
If the net estate as above is <u>under £5,000</u> [see example 2 below].	No fee
Application for a second grant in an estate where a previous grant has been issued.	£15
Additional Copies Official [sealed] copies of the Grant of Representation <u>if</u> ordered when you lodge your application for a Grant of Representation. **N.B. You should decide how many copies you will need and add the cost to your application fee – this will give you the total amount payable. See examples below.** **It can save you a lot of time when collecting in the deceased's assets if you have a few extra copies of the grant to produce to the organisations holding the assets.**	£1 per copy
'Sealed and certified copy' – if assets are held abroad you may need one of these. Please check with the appropriate organisations.	£1 per copy [including Will and Grant]
Additional copies [consisting of grant including a copy of the Will, if applicable] ordered after the Grant of Representation has been issued.	£5 for first copy then £1 per additional copy.

Example 1			**Example 2**		
Net estate of £75,000	= Fee	£90	Net estate of £2,000	= Fee	Nil
4 copies of grant at £1 each	= Fee	£ 4	1 copy of grant at £1 each	= Fee	£1
	Total Fee	£94		Total Fee	£1

Please send a cheque or postal order [NO CASH] made payable to **"H. M. Courts Service"**, together with your application forms, to the Probate Registry to which you are applying. You should state the number and type of copies you need on the checklist on page 4 of the PA1 [application form]. Please print the name of the <u>deceased person</u> on the back of the cheque.

Please ensure you order sufficient copies for your needs, when you send in your application.

Please note: **Appropriate postage must be paid.** (Standard rate postage may not be sufficient. If your forms weigh over 60g they may need to be weighed at your local Post Office).

Fee Refunds/Remissions
If you consider that you would suffer financial hardship if you pay a court fee you can apply for remission (or if you have already paid a fee a refund of that fee or part thereof). If you wish to make such an application you should ask a member of the Registry staff to supply you with form EX160 (including form EX160A). Please note that **fee exemption**, as described in that booklet, does not apply with regard to non-contentious probate fees.

<u>**YOUR APPLICATION WILL NOT BE PROCESSED UNTIL THE FEE IS PAID**</u> (or an application for refund/remission has been successful)

PA3 - Fees revised 4th January 2005   *(04/05)*

Directory of Probate Registries and Interview Venues

Controlling Probate Registries (except **London & Middlesbrough**, see over) are open to the public 9:30am to 4:00pm Monday-Friday.

You can choose any venue for your interview appointment, but your application forms **must** be sent to the Controlling Probate Registry responsible for that venue.

Interview locations, other than Probate Registries, have limited opening times. When selecting such a venue your interview will be fixed for the next available date .If, when you receive notification of that date, you require an earlier interview, you should telephone the controlling registry (phone number will be supplied at that time) to see if an earlier date, at the controlling Registry can be arranged.

Text phone number for the deaf or hard of hearing: **18001 020 7947 7389**

Controlling Probate Registry	Interview Venues	Controlling Probate Registry	Interview Venues
Bangor Probate Sub-Registry Council Offices Ffordd Gwynedd Bangor Gwynedd LL57 1DT Tel: 01248 362410	Bangor Rhyl Wrexham	**Carmarthen Probate Sub-Registry** 14 King Street Carmarthen SA31 1BL Tel: 01267 236238	Carmarthen Aberystwyth Haverfordwest Swansea
Birmingham District Probate Registry The Priory Courts 33 Bull Street Birmingham B4 6DU Tel: 0121 681 3400/3414	Birmingham Coventry Kidderminster Northampton Wolverhampton	**Chester Probate Sub-Registry** 5th Floor Hamilton House Hamilton Place Chester CH1 2DA Tel: 01244 345082	Chester
Bodmin Probate Sub-Registry Market Street Bodmin PL31 2JW Tel: 01208 72279	Bodmin Plymouth Truro	**Exeter Probate Sub-Registry** 2nd Floor Exeter Crown & County Courts Southernhay Gardens Exeter Devon EX1 1UH Tel: 01392 415370	Exeter Barnstaple Taunton Torquay/Newton Abbot Yeovil
Brighton District Probate Registry William Street Brighton BN2 2LG Tel: 01273 573510	Brighton Chichester Hastings Horsham	**Gloucester Probate Sub-Registry** 2nd Floor Combined Court Building Kimbrose Way Gloucester GL1 2DG Tel: 01452 834966	Gloucester Cheltenham Hereford Worcester
Bristol District Probate Registry Ground Floor The Crescent Centre Temple Back Bristol BS1 6EP Tel: 0117 927 3915/926 4619	Bristol Bath Weston-Super-Mare	**Ipswich District Probate Registry** Ground Floor 8 Arcade Street Ipswich IP1 1EJ Tel: 01473 284260	Ipswich Chelmsford Colchester
Cardiff Probate Registry of Wales PO Box 474 2 Park Street Cardiff CF10 1TB Tel: 02920 376479	Cardiff Bridgend Newport Pontypridd	**Lancaster Probate Sub-Registry** Mitre House Church Street Lancaster LA1 1HE Tel: 01524 36625	Lancaster Barrow-In-Furness Blackpool Preston St Helens
Carlisle Probate Sub-Registry Courts Of Justice Earl Street Carlisle CA1 1DJ Tel: 01228 521751	Carlisle	**Leeds District Probate Registry** 3rd Floor, Coronet House Queen Street Leeds LS1 2BA Tel: 0113 386 3540	Leeds

You can choose any venue for your interview appointment, <u>but your application forms</u> **must** <u>be sent to the Controlling Probate Registry for that venue.</u>

Controlling Probate Registry	Interview Venues	Controlling Probate Registry	Interview Venues
Leicester Probate Sub-Registry Crown Court Building 90 Wellington Street Leicester LE1 6HG Tel: 0116 285 3380	Leicester Bedford	**Norwich Probate Sub-Registry** Combined Court Building The Law Courts Bishopgate Norwich NR3 1UR Tel: 01603 728267	Norwich Kings Lynn Lowestoft
Lincoln Probate Sub-Registry 360 High Street Lincoln LN5 7PS Tel: 01522 523648	Lincoln	**Nottingham Probate Sub-Registry** Butt Dyke House 33 Park Row Nottingham NG1 6GR Tel: 0115 941 4288	Nottingham
Liverpool District Probate Registry The Queen Elizabeth II Law Courts Derby Square Liverpool L2 1XA 0151 236 8264	Liverpool Southport	**Oxford District Probate Registry** Combined Court Building St. Aldates Oxford OX1 1LY Tel: 01865 793055	Oxford Aylesbury High Wycombe Reading Slough Swindon
London Probate Department Principal Registry of the Family Division First Avenue House 42-49 High Holborn London WC1V 6NP Tel: 020 7947 6939 Open10.00am-4.30pm Mon-Fri	London Croydon Edmonton Harlow Kingston Luton Southend-on-Sea Woolwich	**Peterborough Probate Sub-Registry** 1st Floor Crown Building Rivergate Peterborough PE1 1EJ Tel: 01733 562802	Peterborough Cambridge
Maidstone Probate Sub-Registry The Law Courts Barker Road Maidstone ME16 8EQ Tel: 01622 202048	Maidstone Canterbury Tunbridge Wells	**Sheffield Probate Sub-Registry** PO Box 832 The Law Courts 50 West Bar Sheffield S3 8YR Tel: 0114 281 2596	Sheffield
Manchester District Probate Registry 9th Floor, Astley House 23 Quay Street Manchester M3 4AT Tel: 0161 837 6070	Manchester Bolton Nelson Oldham Warrington Wigan	**Stoke-on-Trent Probate Sub-Registry** Combined Court Centre Bethesda Street Hanley Stoke-on-Trent ST1 3BP Tel: 01782 854065	Stoke-on-Trent Crewe Shrewsbury Stafford
Middlesbrough Probate Sub-Registry Combined Court Centre Russell Street Middlesbrough TS1 2AE Open: Contact Newcastle DPR for the opening hours	Middlesbrough	**Winchester District Probate Registry** 4th Floor, Cromwell House Andover Road Winchester SO23 7EW Tel: 01962 897029	Winchester Basingstoke Bournemouth Dorchester Guildford Newport I.O.W. Portsmouth Salisbury Southampton
Newcastle-Upon-Tyne District Probate Registry 2nd Floor, Plummer House Croft Street Newcastle-upon-Tyne NE1 6NP Tel: 0191 261 8383	Newcastle-upon-Tyne Darlington	**York Probate Sub-Registry** 1st Floor, Castle Chambers Clifford Street York YO1 9RG Tel: 01904 666777	York Hull Scarborough

PA 4

03/05

My probate appointment - What will happen?

Why do I need to come for an appointment?

The appointment is to confirm the information that you have sent us in your application, which will enable the Probate Service to issue a Grant of Representation. This grant will authorise you to deal with the estate of the deceased person. The appointment will also give you the opportunity to ask any questions you may have.

Where will the appointment take place?

The appointment will be held at the venue indicated on your appointment letter – if this is incorrect, please contact us. The appointment will be in a private room. You will not have to go into a courtroom.

Please follow the instructions on the reverse of your appointment letter and ensure you arrive 10 minutes before the time of the appointment so you do not cause delay to others.

Who is the appointment with?

The appointment will be informal and will be with a member of staff from the Probate Service, who is called a Commissioner. You will not have to see a judge.

How long will the appointment last?

The appointment should last no longer than 15 minutes.

What facilities are available?

Please see your letter of appointment for specific details. If you have any special needs, please contact the Registry to which you sent your application before the date of the appointment.

May I bring a friend or relative with me?

Yes, you are welcome to do so.

Page 1

Do I need to bring any identification with me?

Yes – each personal applicant should bring with them to the interview two separate forms of identification from the following list:-

- Full driving licence
- Passport
- Official bus pass
- National insurance card or National Health card
- State pension book
- Child benefit book
- A letter or invoice from a utilities company.

If you do not have any of the above, please contact us before your interview.

What else do I need to bring?

If we have asked you to bring any documents with you to the appointment, please don't forget them or your appointment may need to be re-arranged for another day. You do not need to bring any other documents such as bank statements etc.

If you wear glasses for reading please bring them.

What will happen at the appointment?

You will be asked to read through a document, referred to as 'The Oath', which we will have prepared from the information you have already given us in your application form.

You will then be asked to confirm that the information in that document is correct, to the best of your knowledge.

Next you will be asked to swear on the New Testament that the contents of The Oath are true.

If you do not want to swear on the New Testament you may either:-

- make an affirmation (which means to make a legal declaration) that the contents are true,

or

- swear on another religious book. If you wish to do this, please contact the office at the top of your appointment letter, before the day of your appointment.

Will I be given the grant at the appointment?

No. It will be posted to you, by second class post, usually within 10 working days of your appointment, together with any copies for which you have paid.

If Inheritance Tax is payable, the grant, and copies, will be posted to you when the Capital Taxes Office has confirmed that it is satisfied the Grant of Representation can be issued.

Any queries regarding Inheritance Tax should be made to the Capital Taxes Office (Helpline – 0845 3020900) (calls charged at local rate).

Which documents will I get back?

The Death Certifcate and, where appropriate, HM Revenue and Customs Account form will be returned to you after the appointment.

The original Will of the deceased will not be returned to you. You will receive an official copy of the Will with the Grant of Representation. The original Will is kept by the Probate Registry and becomes part of public records.

> Please note that we cannot give any legal advice about, for example, the distribution of an estate. You may need to speak to a solicitor/legal adviser or visit a Citizens Advice Bureau.

PA6 My probate appointment - what will happen? (07.05)

Page 3
HMCS

85

Schedule of Standard Probate Letters

(See overleaf)

1.   Letter to Debtors

2.   Letter to Creditors

3.   Letter to Bank applying for payment of Funeral Account

4.   Letter to Bank applying for payment of Inheritance Tax

5.   Letter to Capital Taxes re Inheritance Tax

6.   Letter to Probate Registry for Grant of Probate

7.   Letter to Bank or Building Society collecting funds

8.   Authority for receiving money

9.   Letter to Registrar to transfer shares

10.   Letter paying bills from the Estate

11.   Letter to Beneficiaries with statement for approval

12.   Letter sending Pecuniary Legacy

13.   Receipt for Pecuniary Legacy *(on behalf of ....)*

14.   Receipt for Pecuniary Legacy

15.   Letter to Beneficiary

16.   Receipt for Beneficiary

17.   Instruction sheet for a Will

STANDARD LETTERS

1.   Letter to Debtors

6 September, 2005

Address

Dear Sirs

Re   *Name* – deceased
        Description
        Account No:

We enclose certified copy of the Death Certificate of the above and should be obliged if you would let us know the amount outstanding to the credit of this account including interest accrued but not credited at the date of death.

Probate will be registered with you in due course.

If you have any form or if you require authority for the Executors to sign to let us have any proceeds, repayments or monies due to the Estate could you please let us have such forms.

Alternatively please confirm at this stage exactly what authority you will require. This should save delays once Probate has been granted.

Yours faithfully

2.   Letter to Creditors

6 September, 2005

Customer Services
Address

Dear Sirs

**Re   *Name*   –   deceased
Account Number:**

We act on behalf of the Estate of the above unfortunately
....   died   on   the
.... we enclose a copy of the death certificate for your
information and retention.

We would be obliged if you would kindly forward all future
accounts to ourselves. We are currently making application for
Probate, once this is available we will pay all outstanding
accounts.

Yours faithfully

3.   Letter to Bank Applying for Payment of Funeral Account

6 September, 2005

Bank/Building Society
Address

Dear Sirs

**Re   *Name*   –   deceased
        Address:
        Account No:**

As you are aware we act on behalf of the Estate of the Late
....

We enclose a copy of the funeral account and we would be obliged if it is at all possible for you to draw a cheque in favour of .... to pay this account. If you require any forms to be signed by our client please do not hesitate to contact us.

Your assistance is appreciated

Yours faithfully

4. Letter to Bank applying for payment of Inheritance Tax

6 September, 2005

Bank
Address

Dear Sirs

Re .... – **deceased**
     Account No: ....

As you are aware we act for the Estate of the Late
....

There is a small amount of £........... due for Inheritance Tax and we would be obliged if it is at all possible for you to draw a cheque in favour of the Inland Revenue to pay the amount due.

If you require any forms to be signed by the Executors please do not hesitate to contact us.

Your assistance is appreciated.

Yours faithfully

5. Letter to Capital Taxes re Inheritance Tax

6 September, 2005

Capital Taxes Offices
Section K
Ferres House
PO Box 38
Castle Meadow Road
Nottingham NG2 1BB

Dear Sirs

Re *Name* **– deceased**

We take this opportunity of enclosing the following:

1. A cheque in the sum of £??????? - the total amount of Inheritance Tax due

2. IHT200

3. D1

4. D7

5. D10

6. D13

7. D17

8. D18

We would be obliged if the D18 could be receipted and returned to us in due course.

Yours faithfully

6. Letter to Probate Registry for Grant of Probate

6 September, 2005

Ipswich District Probate Registry
8 Arcade Street
Ipswich
Suffolk IP1 1EJ

Dear Sirs

Re   Name – deceased

We enclose the following to lead to a Grant of Probate of the will of the above:

1.   Oath for Executors

2.   Will dated ?????

3.   *Form IHT205 signed by the Executors*

       or

4.   *D18*

5.   Cheque in the sum of £????

We await hearing from you once Probate has been granted.

Yours faithfully

7.   <u>Letter to Bank or Building Society Collecting Funds</u>

6 September, 2005
Bank/Building Society
Address

Dear Sirs

Re   *Name*   —   **deceased**
         Account No: ....

We take this opportunity of enclosing the following:

1.   Office Copy Probate – kindly return as soon as possible

2.   Authority Letter/Withdrawal form

We await hearing from you with the proceeds of the account.

Yours faithfully

8.   Authority for Receiving Money

6 September, 2005

Bank plc
Address

Dear Sirs

Re *Name* — deceased
    Address
    Account No: **Sort** **Code:**
    Account No: **Sort Code:**

We hereby give you authority to let .... of
.... have the proceeds due to the Estate of
the Late ....

Signature   ....
                            Name:

Signature   ....
                            Name:

Signature   ....
                            Name:

Dated   ....

9.   Letter to Registrar to Transfer Shares

6 September, 2005

Registrars
Address

Dear Sirs

Re   *Name*   –   **deceased**
        .... **Shares**

We take this opportunity of enclosing the following:

1. Original Share Certificate

2. Stock Transfer Form duly signed by the Executors of the Estate

3. Office Copy Probate – Please return as soon as possible

We would be obliged if the Shares could be transferred into the name of ....

Kindly confirm to us when this has been completed.

Yours faithfully

10.   Letter paying bills from the Estate

06/09/2005

Address

Dear Sirs

Re   *Name*   –   **deceased**
       Account Ref:

We take this opportunity of enclosing your account together with a cheque in the sum of £..............

Kindly return your account duly receipted in due course and we would be obliged if you would kindly confirm that there are no further outstanding sums and this account is clear.

Yours faithfully

11.   Letter to Beneficiary with Statement for Approval

6 September, 2005

Beneficiary Name
Address

Dear ....

Re   *Name* – deceased

I take this opportunity of enclosing my statement of account. You will note that there is a retention of £............ which I will hold until I have confirmation that there are no further amounts due from the Estate.

If you would kindly confirm that the statement is in order I will arrange for your share of the residuary Estate to be paid to you immediately.

Yours sincerely

12.   Letter Sending Pecuniary Legacy

6 September, 2005

Address

Dear ....

Re   *Name* – deceased
Address:

We act for the Estate of .... deceased. *Name of deceased* left you a legacy of £........... and we have pleasure in enclosing a cheque for that amount together with a receipt which please sign, date and return to me

Yours sincerely

<u>13.</u>   <u>Receipt for Pecuniary Legacy *(on behalf of* ....*)*</u>

IN THE ESTATE OF .... **- DECEASED**

I .... the Treasurer of
.............., *Address* acknowledge to have received from the
Executors of *Name* deceased the sum of .... Thousand
.... Hundred and .... Pounds (£.........) being the
pecuniary legacy bequeathed to the .... by his / her Will.

Dated   2005

Signed ....

14. Receipt for Pecuniary Legacy

IN THE ESTATE OF .... - DECEASED

I .... acknowledge to have received from the Executors of .... deceased the sum of .... Thousand .... Hundred and .... Pounds and (£...............) being the pecuniary legacy bequeathed to me by his / her Will.

Dated   2005

Signed ....

15.　Letter to Beneficiary

6 September, 2005

Address

Dear ……………...

Re　*Name* – **deceased**

I take this opportunity of enclosing a cheque in the sum of £.……….. which is the amount due to you as one of the beneficiaries of the Estate. *I am holding a small retention of £*……… *for* ……………..

I also enclose a copy of the statement for your information and a receipt which please sign, date and return to me

Yours sincerely

16. Receipt for Beneficiary

IN THE ESTATE OF .... - DECEASED

I .... acknowledge to have received from the
Executors   of
.... deceased the sum of .... Pounds and
.... Pence (£................) being the share of the
residuary Estate bequeathed to me by his / her Will.

Dated   2005

Signed ....

17.   Instruction Sheet for a Will

Full Name: ....

Address: ....

....

Telephone No: ....

Executors: ....

Addresses: ....

Alternative Executors: ....

Addresses: ....

Beneficiaries: ....

....

Addresses: ....

....

(If the Beneficiaries are currently older than you, you may give consideration to appointing an alternative Beneficiary)

Alternative Beneficiaries: ....

Addresses   ....

Any Specific Item you wish to give away: ....

....

Any Specific Sums of Money you wish to give away: ....

....

....

Any other wishes you may have (such as either being buried or cremated)

....

....

....

Signed: ....

Dated: ....

GLOSSARY

A

Abatement :

When the Estate has insufficient money to pay the bills, then any gifts will be reduced pro rata to make enough money to pay such bills, debts and expenses.

Ademption:

If when the Will comes into effect, that is the date of the death, the gift does not exist, the gift lapses. It may have been sold or given away during the deceased's lifetime.

Administrator/Administrix:

In the event of an Intestacy, this is a definition of a person who deals with the deceased's estate.

Assent:

A document which transfer the freehold or leasehold property to the beneficiary.

Assets:

Everything belonging to the deceased

Attestation Clause

A note at the end of the Will, confirming that the Will has been properly signed and witnessed.

B

Bankruptcy

When a person cannot pay their debts, they can apply to the Court to have themselves made bankrupt or you can make someone else bankrupt if you are a creditor. The bankrupts' affairs are then run by the Trustee in bankruptcy until they are discharged.

Beneficiary

Anyone who received assets under the Will.

Bequeathed

Old fashioned word meaning – To leave someone property, more likely now to be bequest. A gift other than cash can be money or shares or other physical items.

Bona Vacantia

In the event of no other relative being alive, there is no one to inherit it goes to the Crown

C

Capacity

This means both mental and being of age that is 18 years old to be able to act as Executor or Administrator and a Beneficiary needs capacity to be able to receive the gift and give a valid receipt.

Capital Gains Tax (CGT)

When an asset has been owned during the deceased's lifetime and is sold for more than it was acquired for, then after deduction of allowances and reliefs, this tax is payable.

Caveat:

A caution which will be given to the Probate Registry when there is doubt about the validity of the Will or whether there is a dispute about who is entitled to be the Executor.

Chargeable Gift

Anything left under the terms of the Will or during a person's lifetime, which is liable to tax.

Chattels

These are such things as pets, cars, boats, furniture, jewellery ornaments etc.   Business assets money and securities are not chattels.

Children

The covers both legitimate and illegitimate children together with. legally adopted children. This does not included stepchildren.

Codicil

An additional Will to make changes in your original Will.

Contentious Probate

Where someone lodges a caveat preventing the issue of a grant and their objections over such matters as the validity of the Will or the entitlement of someone to apply for the grant.

Continent Gift

Something left with a condition attached, which is an age or a condition.

Conveyancing

The process by which land and buildings are transferred.

Court of Protection

Any Power of Attorney either registered or unregistered or the persons affairs were with the Receivers then all such powers lapse on death.

D

Death Certificate

When a death is registered you should obtain extra copies for anyone who needs them.

Most institutions want to see the original copy, not a photocopy.

Devise

Old fashioned word meaning to give

Deeds of Variation

If all the beneficiaries agree, then after the death, the terms of the Will may be altered, usually for the purpose of saving Inheritance Tax. It has to be drawn up within two years of the date of death.

Distribution of the Estate

Once probate has been granted, and all monies have been collected it, all debts and taxes have been paid and the accounts agreed, then the Estate may be distributed.

Donation of Organs

The deceased may give directions for the disposal of their body. The decision is that of the Executors who will generally follow the wishes of the deceased

E

Enduring Power of Attorney (EPOA)

If an Enduring Power of Attorney was being used prior to death this will cease on death.

Engrossment

A final copy of a document.

Excepted Estate

These are estates under a certain limit that do not have to be notified to the Inland Revenue

Executor/Executrix

The Person named in the Will to deal with the deceased Estate.

G

Grant of Letter of Administration

This means the dealing with the deceased's Estate after death. The administration is undertaken by an Administrator, if there is no Will or an Executor if there is a Will.

Grant of Probate

This is where there is a Will and an Executor has been appointed.

Guardians

People appointed by the Will, another parent or the Court to act with parental responsibility for a child.

H

Half Blood

Where people share only one parent in common, they are of the half blood. For example Brother of the half blood.

Headstones

Reasonable costs of the headstone can be deducted with the funeral from the Estate together with reasonable cost of the wake. Again, depending on the size of the Estate.

I

IHT

Inheritance Tax

Intestacy

Where no Will has been made

Intestate

The person who Dies without making a Will

Issue

Or living descendant

J

Joint Tenant

Usually the surviving spouse and the property automatically passes to the surviving spouse and there is an Inheritance Tax exemption.

Joint Assets

Two or more persons have a legal interest in a property, usually land and buildings. Normally, all the other joint owners inherit automatically. They are assessed for Inheritance Tax purposes, even though they pass automatically to the surviving joint owners. A proper valuation should be made.

L

Land Registry

Land Registry www.landreg.gov.uk.

Leasehold property;

The Executor/Administrator retains any rights that the original Leaseholder would have had, such as being able to buy the freehold etc.

Legacy

A gift left to someone in a Will other than house or land.

Letter of Administration

Equivalent to the Grant of Probate where no Will has been made

Liabilities:

Another word for debts. They need to be identified and show in any probate application. Any creditors will need to be informed and once funds have been gathered these debts should be paid off.

Life Interest

The right to enjoy the benefit for life.

M

Minor/Infant

Any child under the age of 18

N

Newspaper Advertisements

These involve Obituary Notices and Trustee Act Notices

O

Oath

An oath is a sworn statement, usually whilst holding the Bible but an affirmation of the truth can be made instead of swearing on the Bible.

Office Copy Entries

This is evidence of the property title at the Land Registry.

P

Pecuniary Legacy

Any Specific amount of money

Personal Representative

Can mean either the Executor or Administrator, just a general term to cover them both.

Probate

Confirmation that the Will is valid and the Executors have the authority to deal with the Estate

R

Renunciation

The Executor has the right to renounce, which means giving up his or her right to be the Executor. To renounce the Executor needs to sign a Form or Letter of Renunciation, which is then sent to the Probate Registry by the proving Executor

Residue

This is the Estate of the deceased, which remains after distribution to the beneficiaries after payment of all gifts and all taxes, debts etc.

Revocation of Will

This means to cancel any previously written Will. Usually a new Will will revoke a previously written Will or it can be revoked in other ways by destroying it etc.

S

Small Estate

Any Estate under the figure of £5000.00

Specific Legacy

A gift of some specific item such as a physical item – car or an amount of money

Spouse

Old legal term for a Wife or Husband.

Survivorship

Where two or more joint Tenants have outlived the deceased. The joint Tenant then inherits a share of the Estate automatically by survivorship. No probate needs to be proved.

T

Tenant

Either a joint tenant or tenant in common. Confusing to the public as this is nothing to do with leasehold property. Therefore you can be a joint tenant or tenant in common of freehold property.

Tenants in common

This is where property is held by two or more people in different shares. Unless shown otherwise, it will usually be fifty/fifty like joint tenants. If one Tenant dies their share passes according to the Will.

Testamentary expenses

Reasonable costs incurred in the administration of the estate. Professional Executors are unable to receive compensation unless it is specific term of the Will.

Testator/Testatrix

This is a person making the Will. Testatrix is the female form.

Trust

An arrangement to hold property for another. The Trustee is not the legal owner.

Trustees

This is where somebody who is responsible to hold Trust assets on behalf of the beneficiaries.

U

Unregistered Land

Certain areas of land have not been registered as there has been no transfer or other variation of the Title. This is equally as affective as registered land but the Land Registry are changing the rules so within the foreseeable future, all land will become registered.

Undue Influence

Where pressure either mental or physical will be put on a party to do an act against their will.

V

Validity of Will

For a Will to be valid it has to be in writing, signed, witnessed correctly and the Testator has to know he or she is signing.

W

Will

INDEX